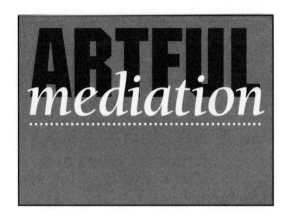

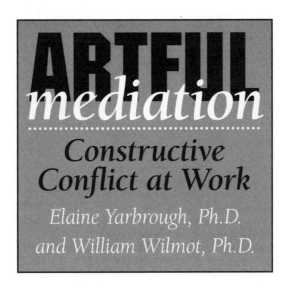

ARTFUL
mediation
Constructive
Conflict at Work

Elaine Yarbrough, Ph.D.
and William Wilmot, Ph.D.

Cairns Publishing
Boulder, Colorado

Cairns Publishing
1113 Spruce Street
Boulder, Colorado 80302
Phone: 303-449-7107
Fax: 303-938-5005

Library of Congress Catalog Card Number: 94-079132

ISBN 0-9643603-0-6

Editor: Diana Somerville
Design: The Mediaworks
Cover: Ed Huston
Photography: Andy Katz

CONTENTS

Chapter 3
Mediation Stage III: Negotiation

Chapter 4
Mediation Stage IV: Agreements

ACKNOWLEDGMENTS

I LOVE HAVING THE CHANCE TO THANK SOME VERY SPECIAL PEOPLE FOR LIVING PEACE and justice in their own ways and giving me a chance to learn from them. As I think about all of them, I see myself in a rich tapestry that weaves together, holding us in grace and beauty.

My deep love and gratitude go to my husband and daughter: Mike Burr and Lindsay Yarbrough Burr. My well-being and growth are grounded with them. In our sixteen years of marriage, Mike has provided a continual presence of peace, fun and gentleness. And above all others, Lindsay offers the reason for hoping so profoundly that we all find ways to live together in harmony. In her generation I see the seeds of future peace — smart young people who see the Earth as a whole once we provide them with a place safe enough to work for interconnection.

My colleagues in Associated Consultants International have been key to my support and my learning for twelve years. To name just a few: Bob Joder who has taught me so much about communication and connection through his work with horses; Anita Sanchez and Kit Tennis who, through their commitment, compassion and creative teaching, alert me to the connection and potential of diversity and conflict; Anne Murray Allen who feels like an indispensable travel companion as we juggle and struggle with our roles as mothers, spouses, friends, professionals and seekers; Bob Rehm, the leader for ACI work in Russia, who never ceases to amaze me with his creative designs and devotion to discovering the common ground from which diverse people can work.

Just as we consultants are hired to teach our clients, we are profoundly taught by them. I want Simon Middleton in Lausanne, Switzerland, a client turned friend, to know how much I have learned from him in terms of clarity of vision and unwavering commitment to the goals of human justice throughout organizations in the world. I also thank him for connecting us with incredible people in his network, people like Peter Gunning from Johannesburg, whose stories about the ongoing work of ordinary people in South Africa have renewed my faith in the extraordinary impact we can have even in the face of massive social injustice.

The Boulder Meeting of Friends has been my spiritual base for the past ten years, allowing and helping me explore the source of strength conflict work requires. A special thank you to Elise Boulding for her continual role modeling of what it means to be a global citizen; to Holly Giffin for her playful, loyal spirit and conflict work with children; to Betty Cannon for her friendship and continued work in matters of human development; and to Mary Hey whose dedication to worship has been inspiring.

And then there are those who extend way back and whose influence is as enduring as the seasons. The faculty members of Skrewe University — Marlene Wilson, Arlene Schindler and Sue Vineyard — are like jewels on a silk Turkish rug. We fly, we meet, we laugh and learn, we navigate the next phase of life.

My heartfelt appreciation to my Dream Group — Alana Shaw, Diana Somerville, Christine Johnson and Barbara Sternberg. They have provided a deeply trusted place for rejuvenation, self-exploration and reconnection to the feminine — all crucial to me. Our exploration of symbols greatly informed my work with metaphors and rituals in conflict and provided an important basis for my international cultural undertakings.

Joyce Hocker, one of the first writers on interpersonal conflict and co-author of what is still the best-selling conflict book in the communication field, is the one who focused my interest in the field. As a dear friend, leader of women's gatherings and godmother to Lindsay, our paths are inextricably joined and my appreciation crosses all boundaries of head and heart.

Bill Wilmot, co-author with Joyce in early work on conflict, associate, friend and godfather to Lindsay, has given me more than I ever could have hoped for in a "university colleague." I carry him in my head always as the voice that says, "People can create amazing solutions, given the chance;" "It's not the personalities, it's the communication;" and "Have you noticed how wonderfully people change when they feel safe?" Thank you, Bill, for believing in me, for supporting me and for being a major catalyst in the field of mediation.

Jim and Lynda Firth teach me what nurturing and abiding friendships are all about. Some tough spots would have been almost impossible without their love. The trust in the inherent goodness of people's processes that Jim brings to our facilitation work has helped me let go as I do my mediation work. His skillful moving of the oars of his raft through river rapids provides me a vivid image I use in mediation, a reminder to use — not fight — the energy of the conflict, to read the currents below the surface and to never underestimate the natural power of the current.

Vicki Hamer, friend since graduate school, office manager for the Yarbrough Group for several years, nanny, cook and resident poet for our six-month stay in Europe, is a spiritual ally who has given so much to me and my family. I have learned much from her transparency, her seeking for community and connection to the Earth and her beautifully written stories about chickens and bugs and plants.

I can't imagine my life without my "brother," Richard Nadeau, whose very way of being in the world is the most amazing combination of setting boundaries and building bridges.

And as I started with my current family, I close with my family of origin. My ninety-seven-year-old grandmother, Alma Green, my mother, Drue Yarbrough, and my sister, Sylvia Netherland, are living, thriving examples of the pioneer women from whence we all come and who have always been the historical grounding for peace issues; my father, Homer Yarbrough, struggled against all odds and survived by his "smarts" and persistence. What a backdrop you have furnished for my life. Thank you.

Elaine Yarbrough

ALL OUR PERSONAL AND PROFESSIONAL PATHS TAKE UNEXPECTED TWISTS AND turns, usually due to fortuitous meetings of others along the way. It was my good fortune to meet Elaine Yarbrough back in 1976, with no idea that she and I would someday work together. Elaine's professionalism, coupled with her unique ability to touch others, has continued to influence me over the decades. Each time I reach a new plateau, I look at her and her work and see another level to be attempted. Thanks, Elaine, for being friend, role model and colleague.

My own evolving ideas about conflict were forged in the context of a multifaceted relationship with Joyce Hocker and I owe her a note of thanks for the early years when we worked on adapting the principles of international conflict management to the family and to organizational contexts.

I'll never forget the amazing impact Will Neville had during my first mediation training session. I had the opportunity to role-play a parent who was invoking rather disgusting behaviors and was really "into" this role, for it contained large shadow parts of me. Will's intervention literally left me speechless — and I learned just how powerful mediation can be. Thanks, Will.

I especially owe a debt of gratitude to the many business owners and management teams, and the supervisors and employees of governmental and non-profit organizations who have presented their struggles to me. It takes a large leap of faith to allow an outsider to come into your midst to try to help. Each time I am given the opportunity to assist others in managing their disputes, I come away with renewed optimism that people can transcend differences and learn to operate in more peaceful, empowering ways.

And, a special thanks to the many individuals who contribute to the growth of the fields of conflict management and mediation by practicing, writing, theorizing and staying with the task. The collective power of all your work is finally being felt in our culture.

Finally, to my children, Carina and Jason, whose lives are unfolding in their own directions now, I take great pride in you and it is good you don't hear all the positive things I say about you to others, so you don't have a chance to disavow them.

Bill Wilmot

PREFACE: WHAT DO WE KNOW ABOUT CONFLICT?

WE ALL KNOW CONFLICT CAN BE ONE OF THE MOST DEVASTATING kinds of human communication. We first encountered it as children, figuring out how to protect ourselves from those bigger than us and experiencing what it felt like trying to get what we wanted while feeling we had little or no real power over our situation.

We all experience conflict as adults in our personal relationships as they move from the honeymoon, where all is light and delight, to power struggles and stages of growth where we must acknowledge how we differ. Who has not pondered how to resolve the seeming contradiction of enjoying being close to someone while occasionally feeling resentment, anger and a need for distance?

We experience conflict in our professional lives as we work to contribute our talents and strengths and encounter those who do things differently or who work toward disparate goals.

We witness a frightening form of conflict on the national and global levels. Violent crime, riots and wars catch us as either participants or observers while the media make it even more difficult to escape witnessing one atrocity after another. We may have been touched deeply, perhaps even personally scarred, by the aftermath of some destructive conflict.

But often, just as we are about to lose hope, something shifts in a wonderful direction. A personal conflict is resolved constructively, restoring intimacy. A work team discovers the underlying issues that had everyone at loggerheads and then breaks through, releasing new creative, productive energy. Or peace breaks out on the global scene. Walls fall, bridges are built between conflicting racial or ethnic groups and old enemies lead whole nations toward a new vision of harmony.

These constructive conflicts on the national or international scene can seem coincidental or even magical, in part because we, as outside observers, have no awareness of the hard behind-the-scenes work that has gone into transforming them. With little or no information on how these shifts come to be it is hard to discern the principles that produce positive results. The perception that such changes are extraordinary is reinforced by our own experience. By the time we reach adulthood, we have already incorporated most of our learnings about the very nature of conflict and developed our own ways of handling it. And, if you are like most people, your education and experiences have given you little information about how to transform life's inevitable conflicts into something creative or liberating.

The skills needed to turn destructive conflict into constructive, life-enhancing experiences can be learned — but even accepting that idea may, for many people, require a leap of faith. In writing this book, we are extending a hand to help those willing to make that leap.

Seeking the Power to Transform

For more than twenty years, our quest has been to discover ways of preventing and reversing the destructive cycle of disputes, transforming them into constructive conflicts. We have encountered ways that work and incorporated the principles underlying them. By teaching other people to use these ideas and methods, we are striving to replace the negative cycle of conflict with a positive pattern and to move the energy and intensity consumed by destructive conflict toward more constructive gains.

Our quest has included examining how people can engage in face-to-face dialogue about their differences in ways that allow them to emerge with workable truths, truths that guide them in solving their problems, reaching their aspirations and building healthier, richer, stronger relationships.

Time and again we see how strong, nurturing relationships ultimately form the basis of vital communities. Our ultimate aim is to reinforce healthy, positive communities at every level of our lives: where we work and in our homes, our neighborhoods, our cities, our nations.

Mediation is a framework that reflects these intentions, a process that focuses on regulating communication so that people in opposition can rise above their polarized viewpoints and see possibilities of being together in mutually supportive ways.

Artful mediation is a process that:

▸ Insists that the means for managing conflict is a key factor in creating workable outcomes.

▸ Steps outside our normal framework of winners and losers — including the adversarial assumptions that underlie our legal system — to demand looking at the truth of all sides.

▸ Seeks to heal relationships grounded in feelings while addressing the problems grounded in facts.

Mediation need not be applied only when problems arise but can also serve as a lens through which to view our ordinary patterns of communication and all of our relationships every day. Mediation is both a set of useful skills and a philosophical approach. It is also a way of being in the world and doing our daily business, a way that sets in motion positive, thriving energy to supplant protective, political, adversarial approaches.

Working Within Organizations

People spend a great deal of their time at work and derive much of their sense of contribution and satisfaction from their working lives. The impact of organizations seems to be growing more pronounced in the last four decades as work becomes far more central to our identities and, in turn, the contexts in which we work influence our ability to form and sustain peaceful relationships in our families and communities.

Thus the context in which we teach people to manage conflict is primarily within organizations, whether those are corporate, governmental or non-profit organizations. We are interested in the process of bringing mediation into all kinds of organizational settings and we work with those inside organizations and those who serve as consultants who come in from the outside.

Most contemporary mediation books focus on family mediation and interpersonal conflict. Their information is necessary, but not sufficient for applying mediation where the elements such as organizational structure, reward systems and cultural norms must be considered in unraveling disputes. When people within an organization act as mediators, whether they are specialists or trusted colleagues, the nature of their organizational position means they will not be seen as neutral and impartial — which are both crucial aspects of mediation. Consequently, we address the special considerations needed to apply mediation as an effective everyday tool inside organizations.

Mediation is both science and art and good mediators have a theoretical framework for making thoughtful interventions and practical skills to embody the framework. As much as we may know from personal experience and theoretical research, the proof still lies in the artful application of its principles. As much as possible, within the framework of a book, we aim to provide you with both a theoretical framework and the practical nuts-and-bolts of using mediation in real-life situations.

Who Can Use This Book?

Artful Mediation is designed primarily for people without extensive backgrounds in communication or dispute resolution. It provides detailed steps for implementing the process, as well as examples drawn from our own experiences, real-life dialogues, useful checklists and general guidelines. We provide all the necessary steps of this fascinating process, but are not attempting to summarize all of the current knowledge and research about mediation. A bibliography provides some guidance for those who wish to explore various aspects of mediation in more depth. *Artful Mediation* may also provide seasoned professionals with ways to refine their understanding and develop additional ideas for enhancing the ways that they conduct their practices.

The principles of *Artful Mediation* can also be useful when you find yourself involved in the conflict. Although as a party in the conflict you will not have the distance or the credibility of someone who is independent and uninvolved, you can use these skills to help transform negative disputes into creative conflict.

All human relationships are connected, so that as we learn to manage conflicts constructively at work, this learning also enriches other parts of our lives as well. Just as a stone tossed into a pond creates ripples that expand into ever wider circles, so each time you transform a negative situation, you expand a more positive way of being in the world.

INTRODUCTION:
THE HOWS, WHYS AND
WHATS OF MEDIATION

Highly qualified scientists had been tapped from a company's divisions worldwide to form a special team to produce a new product. Many were young, high achievers, with little organizational experience. Scant attention was paid to building relationships among the team members, most of whom had been highly recognized individual contributors.

Within months, sub-groups had formed, each one building its cases for why the other sub-groups were incompetent. Trust had deteriorated so badly that factions were withholding vital product development information from one another. The two team leaders were no longer talking to each other and, instead, were siding with their teams.

Meanwhile, back in the parent organization, those who had opposed forming the special team in the first place were taking potshots at the team and its supporters and generally reveling in their feelings of vindication. All the players had lost sight of the fact that a well-timed new product could bolster the stability of the whole organization.

Longtime, loyal employees at a health clinic were alarmed as their previously small operation grew rapidly. They quibbled over small details like where to locate the medical charts and who was responsible for keeping the staff kitchen clean. Gossip was rampant but little attention was paid to official communication. Resentment was high and decisions were slow.

Surface conflicts and organizational symptoms masked the underlying

1

issue — fear that growth would mean a less caring environment. "We don't want to be like a corporation," they maintained. For some, succeeding financially symbolized selling out. A few longtime employees would not change and needed to move on. With the real issues unmanaged, the mission of the clinic — providing health care to patients — was delayed and undermined.

MEDIATION HELPED PARTICIPANTS IN BOTH THESE CONFLICTS TO AIR their resentments. Exploring their goals and interests, they each discovered many that were similar to those of their "opponents." Both the scientists and the clinic staff found ways to revamp parts of their organization to support future collaboration. Successfully meeting a new product deadline was cause for celebration in the company. The clinic now serves more health care clients than ever before in an atmosphere of caring and healing. Mediation allowed each group to negotiate agreements that were beneficial to all the people involved. Each was able to re-commit to its work. Both groups found renewed energy to bring to a newly discovered shared vision.

But such success stories, alas, are far from the norm. In many organizations where conflicts continue to unfold, those involved grow increasingly unproductive as strife consumes more of their energy and distorts their focus. Others find themselves taking sides or withdrawing to stay out of the fray. Among the ingredients of awful conflicts are:

- ‣ Avoiding direct discussion.
- ‣ Wishing the conflict (or the other person) would go away.
- ‣ Forming coalitions with others and complaining about the opposition.
- ‣ Unrelenting rounds of "dirty tricks" to make others look foolish, to diminish their political power or just to get even.
- ‣ Litigation or grievances filed after attempts to solve the conflict don't work.

Locked in awful conflicts, people often need help breaking out of all-too-familiar patterns, sorting out their needs, hearing others in the dispute and creating cooperative solutions. This kind of help can only come from someone outside the dispute. This may be a manager, another person outside the troubled unit or department or a professional mediator or organizational development specialist from outside the organization.

Awful conflicts can be turned around. Their negative energy can be transformed, to allow satisfying, creative outcomes to emerge. But the transformation takes time and skillful attention. We believe mediation offers the most respectful and rewarding framework for managing conflicts and disputes.

Why Mediation?

There are both philosophical and practical reasons for looking to mediation. Let's start with some of the practical aspects.

Mediation reduces the costs to organizations. Time, money and emotional energy are expended in disputes. Both tangible and human resources can be consumed or destroyed. What's more, as we hope to demonstrate, unaddressed or mishandled conflicts all too often represent lost opportunities.

Mediation increases everyone's satisfaction with the outcomes. It is a process that respects all parties equally. People who feel heard, valued and validated are content with the outcomes they themselves have helped to shape and are ready to make a greater commitment to the goals of their organization.

Mediation enhances relationships among people. When people engage fully in the mediation process, it often transforms antagonists into those with a richer appreciation of each individual's contribution to the whole organization.

Mediation reduces the recurrence of conflict. When conflicts don't reappear, organizations reap the benefits in terms of saving resources — time, money, emotional and physical energy. But perhaps more significantly, the mediation process also salvages lost opportunities for dynamic growth and change.[1]

How is the Working World Changing?

Organizations increasingly find themselves operating in a quickly changing milieu, often in a marketplace that is global and vastly more competitive. Hence, the time allowed from product conception to the marketplace is shrinking to near invisibility, to cite but one example of the acceleration. Pushing for greater quality and trying to do more with less create internal organizational pressures. These demands are often met by creating cross-functional and self-managed work teams, which in turn adds further potential for conflict.

Once upon a time, an unresolved issue might simmer for months or even years. Simply ignoring a potent problem allowed managers to avoid the challenges of managing conflict for quite some time. Now, however, slow simmers are being replaced by explosive — and expensive — flash points as accelerated change sets the stage for more openly expressed conflict.

Changes in the workforce itself add to the urgency. Consider the increasing diversity, for instance. The often quoted Hudson Institute Report on *Workforce 2000* predicts that 85 percent of those entering the workforce in this decade will be women, minorities and immigrants.[2] Not only must organizations pull qualified workers from these untraditional labor pools, but they must also learn to manage a diverse workforce that is demanding to be empowered.

Organizations that want to keep pace in this pressure-cooker atmosphere are finding mediation the most effective way to manage internal conflicts. Why? In brief, because today's managers typically spend a third of their time dealing with conflict. When conflicts are mishandled, this means a third of their effort is ultimately wasted. A working environment where conflict continues unchecked not only wastes managerial expertise but destroys people's commitment and saps their creative energy.

Moreover, innovative managers are learning how, properly managed, constructive conflict can be the catalyst for change, improvement and growth. Competitive creativity opens up new opportunities for using the diverse skills and untraditional opinions of an expanded workforce. Organizations that strive to use the resources of all their people, not just those traditionally in power, also reap the benefits of the different perspectives those people bring. To cite but one example, the push toward building relationships with customers and within working teams allows women's interpersonal skills to be tapped productively.

The changing shape of the corporate world plays a role in increasing the potential for conflict that is all too often overlooked. Mergers and acquisitions continue as a strong trend, even though most mergers have only a 50-50 chance of being successful. The most common reason for failure lies in unresolved conflicts sparked by bringing together people from different corporate and/or national cultures.[3]

Forces beyond the workplace contribute to the pressures for change as well. Today's lifestyles grow more complex and demanding. Individuals are increasingly stressed by personal struggles with rearing children in dual-career families, managing blended and extended families and caring for aging parents. Time — including time demanded by the workplace — becomes a more precious, limited resource. Unresolved social problems, from child care to racial discrimination, bring more pressures to bear in the workplace, creating a greater potential for conflicts while increasing the organization's risk of losing valuable human resources. Personal, social and cultural values increasingly overlap and the appropriate role for an organization to play becomes subject to debate.

Time and again organizations discover the hard way that avoiding conflict does not work in the long term. Managing divergence by demanding conformity and using power and coercion to enforce the demand is counterproductive — and ultimately self-defeating. The organizations that adapt to increased complexity and diversity will be the ones that survive and thrive.

Mediation offers a process uniquely able to open up the creative benefits inherent in conflict and structures ways to make these conflicts constructive.

What Exactly Is Mediation?

The word *mediation* sounds formidable. For many people it conjures up images of stern-faced individuals spending days around a large table hammering out minute details of a complex agreement. Happily, such scenes are the exception rather than the rule. Most day-to-day conflicts — whether they erupt between individuals or emerge in a team — can be handled informally, in the natural flow of doing business.

It's important to note that mediation is not the same thing as negotiation, although people often mistakenly assume the terms are interchangeable. Negotiation, as you will see, is only a part of the whole process of mediation.

Fundamentally, mediation is the art of altering the positions of those in dispute, changing their perceptions of each other and of the issues, so that they can manage their differences. In practice, this means a trusted person helps those in conflict to reach agreement.

Successful mediation is grounded in several key assumptions:

▸ Conflict is inevitable — and resolvable.

▸ Conformity is not required. Diversity is valued.

▸ Few situations are hopeless.

▸ Each side has a piece of the truth and a piece of the solution.

▸ There is no one right answer.

▸ There are similarities as well as differences between people in conflict.

▸ History should be acknowledged, but present problems are the ones to solve.[4]

There are significant differences between mediation and the legal system which is the model for handling conflict that most organizations use. The legal system is adversarial. It pits two opponents against each other to determine winners and losers, who's right and who's wrong. The rights of the disputing parties are protected by legal mechanisms such as allowing equal time to present one's case and the right to cross-examine witnesses.

Mediation has no such mechanisms. It insures the rights and protects the feelings of both parties by giving them both equal time to talk and by keeping them focused on the issues at hand. The mediator's tasks are to keep productive communication flowing between the parties and to focus on the problems to be solved, keeping the issues at the forefront.

By contrast, a judge pays no attention to the communication between the disputants. A judge or jury — or complaint officer or manager — listens to testimony, examines evidence and then renders a verdict the parties are supposedly obliged to accept. The disputants, often several steps removed from the process, present their cases indirectly, through attorneys or other professional advocates. Often, a judgment may be handed down without either party talking directly with the other.

When people face an adjudicator who has some form of power over them, their own personal power is diminished and their spectrum of choices is reduced — which also shuts off their creativity and destroys their commitment to the process and its outcomes.

In many an organization, a manager often acts as arbitrator or judge, rendering a decision in ordinary, everyday conflicts. This common practice has several drawbacks. First of all, with no awareness of the mediation process, managers rarely address the feelings generated in the conflict. Even the "winners" are often left with unfocused feelings of dissatisfaction. Resentments linger, because the relationship between those at odds with each other has not been healed but simply stifled. Old wounds left unhealed more easily open up again — setting the stage for future conflicts that often build in intensity with each successive round.

The process of mediation cannot be used in every conflict. The stages of a conflict in which mediation is most effective are shown in the Struggle Spectrum at the end of this chapter. The Struggle Spectrum also notes conditions that can keep a conflict from escalating.

When an outsider helps in the mediation process, the disputants are more likely to see the mediator as neutral and are less likely to feel pressured or coerced in the mediation process. Inside an organization, few if any people are perceived as neutral. Their organizational role comes with some form of power and authority. Consequently, when managers, human resources specialists or other trusted colleagues are cast in the role of mediators, their first order of business must be to establish their neutrality. They must clarify their stakes in the dispute in order to be seen as able and willing to treat all parties in the conflict fairly.

It is a challenge — but one that can be met effectively. We will show you, step by step, how to set up an effective mediation when the mediator and the disputants are members of the same organization. While this situation requires special care and attention, we believe this powerful process can be used with integrity by people within an organization to produce strong agreements.

What Is Required of a Mediator?

Whether the mediation process is used by a professional mediator in a coal strike, by family members in dispute or by managers working with their teams, the process used in conflicts has a dramatic impact on the solution. In short, how well the mediator conducts the process helps determine whether or not the parties reach agreement, the durability of the agreements and the satisfaction of the disputing parties.

Being a successful mediator begins with an overall view of the mediation process. A mediator must have a full spectrum of "soft," receptive skills and "hard," directive skills. The mediation process begins with a soft, receptive approach, characterized by listening, exploration, and empathy. As people are heard and understood, as problems are analyzed, and as negotiation begins, the mediator moves from one stage to the next, using harder, more directive approaches.

Often people with counseling training or those who work in non-profit, helping organizations tend to stay too long in the soft side of the spectrum. They assume that as long as information is gathered and people are given a chance to be heard, the disputants will grow to like each other and the problem will melt away. They resist assuming more directive approaches and shy away from seeking clear, crisp agreements that can be tracked and followed.

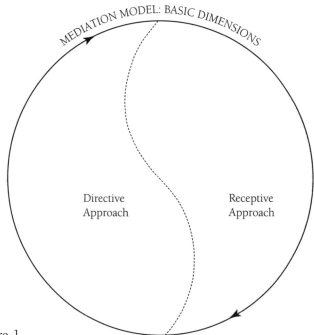

Figure 1

By contrast, people who work in fast-paced industries often think they must drive a hard bargain. They tend to overlook the steps toward mutual understanding and skip the time-consuming process of gathering diagnostic information. They go for the tough deal. This approach often lowers trust, creates resentment and sets the stage for a hard bargaining cycle that wastes time and consumes resources.

What Is Involved in the Mediation Process?

Mediation focuses on:

▸ Behavior that can be changed, not on personalities.

▸ Real versus surface issues.

▸ Control of the communication process more than the outcome.

▸ The skills the disputants use to help them make their own decisions.

▸ Reaching mutual, workable and legally sound agreements.

Mediation is a five-stage process and each stage requires certain methods and skills. The stages are:

1. Entry

2. Diagnosis

3. Negotiation

4. Agreements

5. Follow-up

What is involved in each stage is detailed in subsequent chapters. But the process itself is a cycle best represented by what we call the Mediation Wheel.

The Mediation Wheel presents the components of each stage of mediation and their relationship with each other. We offer it as a guide to help you in planning and conducting the specifics of mediation.

We have designed this book to follow each turn of the wheel. We explain how to enter into the mediation process, how to diagnose the issues, the skills of negotiation, the characteristics of agreements and what sort of follow-up is appropriate. We introduce the principles involved in each phase, provide examples and case studies to aid you in using the principles.

As you follow the stages of the mediation process, moving from one part of the wheel to the next, keep in mind the following general principles.

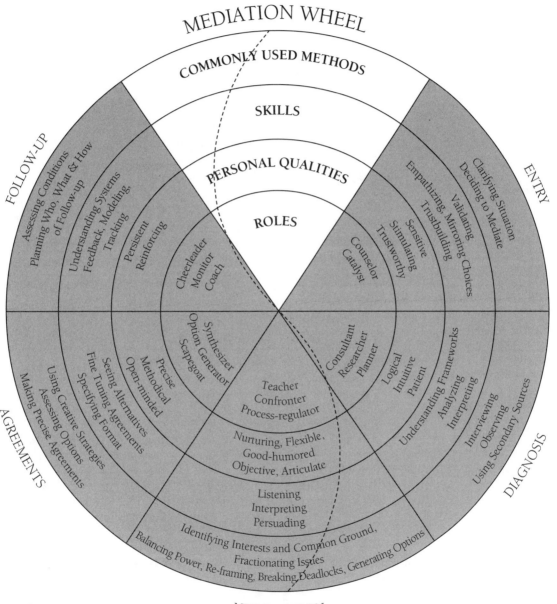

Figure 2

Mediation is embedded in an organizational context

The mediator must be aware that organizational pressures need to be examined. Sometimes organizational issues can masquerade as interpersonal conflict. Consider the example of a telephone company that had so much bickering among its customer service representatives that the supervisor asked for help in mediating these conflicts. A detailed diagnosis uncovered several significant facts. First of all, the job of the customer service representative — answering angry calls the entire day — was stressful in itself. Each representative worked alone, thus adding isolation to the anger each individual had to cope with on a daily basis.

To make matters worse, the company rewarded representatives based on the number of calls they answered in a day and the degree to which each angry customer was satisfied after the call. The first criterion all too often cancelled out the second. Representatives were constantly forced to choose between quantity and quality in their interactions with customers. The company's reward system added another level of stress and internal conflict to an already stressful job.

The customer service representatives needed a chance to communicate regularly with co-workers on their team, not just angry customers. And they needed a logically consistent reward system. As a matter of fact, when those things were changed, the supervisor was surprised to discover that most of the interpersonal conflict evaporated.

Organizational pressures may be key components of any dispute. The mediator may need to take into account any number of systems issues in order to diagnose conflicts accurately and decide how to intervene. The organizational culture, the structure of the work, the leadership, the reward system and the existing conflict management procedures may all play a part. Moreover, each organization functions in a larger economic and cultural environment. See figure 3, page 15. The chapter on Diagnosis provides more detailed information on examining organizational conditions.

If you miss a phase of mediation, agreements either will not be reached or will not endure

A Board President, wanting to settle a dispute between a new Director and a longtime, valued Employee, brought both people together to work things out. The Employee, several levels down in the organization, felt neither safe nor understood. Frightened or intimidated by meeting with the Board President and the Director, she verbally agreed with the Director's wishes. But after their meeting, she dragged her feet and managed to stayed confused about the agreement.

The Director first felt victorious. But his feeling of triumph after the meeting soon turned to confusion and anger when he found that "even in my position, I can't get anything done around here."

Here, the Board President's mistake was skipping the entry stage and going directly to negotiation. He did not first make certain that both the Director and the Employee accepted the process and his role in it, or that they were fully committed to the agreements — not simply paying lip service. Also, by assuming he understood all the circumstances clearly, the Board President omitted the information gathering required in the diagnosis stage. Thus, he failed to have a clear grasp of the issues between the Director, who needed support, and the Employee, whose underlying concern was job security. Sometimes, when the issues are clearly understood, the terms that need to be negotiated become obvious.

The overall approach needs to be in alignment with the stage of mediation you are in

What happens when two employees are at each other's throats while the outcome of a project depends on their cooperation? Their manager doesn't want to be bothered with details and just wants everybody to get on with their work. Instead of listening patiently, the manager may try to persuade the angry parties to cooperate and then suggest a solution. Without a full understanding of the issues, the manager mandates a solution that, in fact, works for neither of the disputing parties. Both employees may acquiesce initially, agree to the manager's solution and return to work. Soon, however, they will revert to their old patterns of disagreement. Or they may find new, perhaps even more disruptive ways to act out their conflicts.

By simply wanting to get things settled so everyone would return to work, the manager made the mistake of using persuasion as a key skill early on in a dispute, in what should have been the diagnosis stage of the conflict. To be powerful and effective in the diagnostic stage, the manager needed to listen carefully and track the issues from the disputants' perspectives.

This book can provide a map for a journey of discovery, a gateway into experiencing the transformative power of mediation. We see mediation as both a set of skills and a philosophical approach. Time and time again, we have found positive energy thriving beneath the surface of conflict.

Any organization that fully commits to the mediation process will find itself moving away from the more traditional ways of doing things, which are often forms of coercion in disguise. Yet taking the path toward valuing all the individuals who make up an organization and the contributions each can make will enhance all the people, their work and the organization itself. We intend this book to be a useful, trustworthy guide to that path. Those who follow it will, we believe, find their working lives, their organizations and their overall creativity enriched by the journey.

Figure 3

For successful mediation, what you are doing and how you are doing it — the methods, skills, personal qualities and roles — must fit with each stage of the process. You need to be aware of each successive stage, completing one process before moving on to the next. Then you will be able to reap the benefits of mediation — strong agreements that actually work in the organization and individuals who feel valued by the mediation process.

APPLICATION

▸ The **Struggle Spectrum** shows how conflicts tend to escalate, moving from differences to disputes to litigation to war. It can also serve as a reminder of ways to keep a conflict contained within reasonable limits.

The Struggle Spectrum:
From Differences to Disputes

When issues are not resolved at one stage the tendency is to move to the right on the continuum. Parties lose their joint decision-making power when mediation is no longer available.

	Stage 1 ⟶ Mild Difference	Stage 2 ⟶ Disagreement	Stage 3 ⟶ Dispute
Processes	Discussion	Discussion Negotation	Argument Bargaining
Behavior	Joint problem solving	Contentions over choices	Rational proof & game playing by rules
Relationships	Partners, friends & acquaintances	Rivals	Opponents
Goals	Includes other	Includes other	Excludes other
Orientation to Each Other	Cooperative & amicable	Disputative Conciliatory	Win/lose (1) Hostile
Communication	Open & friendly	Open but strained	Limited Tense
Decision Making	Mutual decisions	Joint decisions & agreements	Joint decisions in mediation Third-party decisions in arbitration
Intervention Possibilities	None needed	Mediation by neutral party	Mediation or arbitration by neutral party
Possible Outcomes	Integrated agreement satisfaction	Accommodated agreement Both pacified	Compromise agreement or one wins

Notes: 1. Mediation most appropriate in stages 2 and 3, is relatively useless in Stages 1, 4, 5 and 6, but may be used in 4 under special arrangement.
2. Win/lose escalates from Stages 3 to 5. The longer it exists the more intense it becomes.
3. Neutral third parties have no stake in the outcome of the struggle and include mediators, arbitrators, judges and juries.

to Litigation to War

Stage 4 → Campaign	Stage 5 → Litigation	Stage 6 Fight or War	
Persuasion Pressure	Advocacy Debate	Violent conflict	**Processes**
Emotional & logical strategies	Selective proofs before judges or juries	Psychological and/or physical violence	**Behavior**
Competitors	Antagonists	Enemies	**Relationships**
Excludes other	Excludes other	Eliminates other	**Goals**
Win/lose (2) Estranged	Win/lose (3) Alienated	Irreconcilable	**Orientation to Each Other**
Restricted & planned Antagonistic	Blocked & controlled Hostile	Closed except for violence	**Communication**
Vote by constituents or third-party decisions	Third-party court- room decisions by judge or jury	Each side seeks control by forcing other	**Decision Making**
Arbitration by neutral party or election vote	Arbitration or judge or jury	Force of police or other military intervention	**Intervention Possibilities**
A win or draw Winner pleased Loser accepting	One wins Winner celebrates	One prevails Other or both destroyed or harmed	**Possible Outcomes**

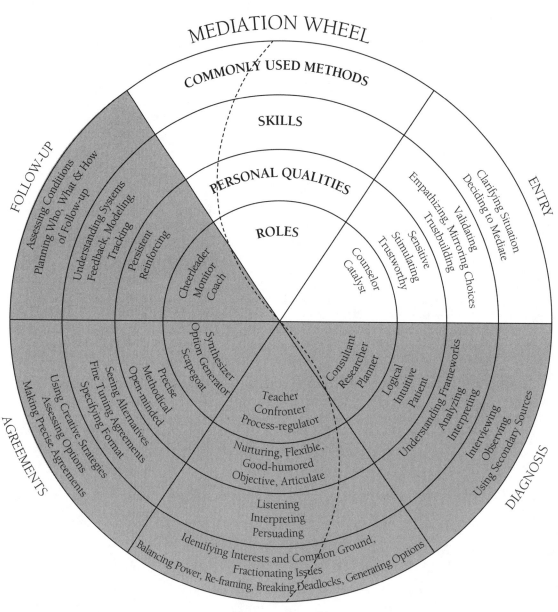

MEDIATION WHEEL

COMMONLY USED METHODS

SKILLS

PERSONAL QUALITIES

ROLES

ENTRY

Clarifying Situation
Deciding to Mediate

Validating
Empathizing, Mirroring Choices
Trustbuilding

Sensitive
Stimulating
Trustworthy

Counselor
Catalyst

DIAGNOSIS

Interviewing
Observing
Using Secondary Sources

Understanding Frameworks
Analyzing
Interpreting

Logical
Intuitive
Patient

Consultant
Researcher
Planner

NEGOTIATION

Balancing Power, Re-framing, Breaking Deadlocks, Generating Options
Identifying Interests and Common Ground,
Fractionating Issues

Listening
Interpreting
Persuading

Nurturing, Flexible,
Good-humored
Objective, Articulate

Teacher
Confronter
Process-regulator

AGREEMENTS

Making Precise Agreements
Assessing Options
Using Creative Strategies
Specifying Format
Fine Tuning Agreements
Seeing Alternatives

Precise
Methodical
Open-minded

Synthesizer
Option Generator
Scapegoat

FOLLOW-UP

Assessing Conditions
Planning Who, What & How
of Follow-up
Understanding Systems
Feedback, Modeling,
Tracking

Persistent
Reinforcing

Cheerleader
Monitor
Coach

MEDIATION STAGE I:
ENTRY INTO THE CONFLICT

Larry, one of five managers in a high tech company, is asked by the CEO to recommend a comprehensive reorganization plan for the divisions. Walking down the hall, he hears John, one of the managers, say to another, "Over my dead body — that's a stupid idea!" Sam, another manager, storms out, slamming John's office door.

John comes to Larry and says, "You've got to join with me on this. Sam is irrational and out of line." The meeting with the CEO is next week.

Susan, in Human Resources, hears persistent rumors that Eileen, a project manager, and Stan, a line manager, are "at war" with one another. Eileen decides to change the destructive patterns and asks Susan, "Is there anything you can do to get Stan to cooperate with me?"

NO DOUBT YOU HAVE BEEN PART OF CONVERSATIONS IN WHICH frustrated people struggle to figure out how to deal with the kinds of interpersonal tensions in the incidents above. And, if you manage others, you likely have spent sleepless nights wondering why competent people could make work so difficult.

Most organizations typically manage conflicts in destructive ways. Both size and organizational structures often make direct communication difficult. An atmosphere charged with fear and a climate of informal political influence can transform the simplest issue into an imagined catastrophe. Often unspoken expectations of what makes a good leader or manager — one who is tough and decisive, who sticks to business and is not sidetracked by human concerns — establish the groundwork for win/lose conflicts. Misinterpretations prevalent in cross-cultural settings or in situations involving gender, age or race differences heat up conflicts.

But even the simplest conflicts generate tension. Consequently, establishing safety for the participants and confidence in the mediation process is critical in the entry phase. If the entry phase is done well, even though tensions are high, disputants will be more likely to speak the truth about their most serious concerns and to support collaborative solutions.

To create safety for the participants and confidence in the process, you need to consider the following:

1. Assessing initial conditions

2. Generating credibility

3. Selecting a conflict approach that fits the problem at hand

4. Indicating your expectations for a successful mediation.

We examine each of these in detail.

Assessing Initial Conditions

The mediation process can be brought into a situation in any number of ways. How the mediation begins, who suggested the process and the relative power of that person and the disputants are all important considerations. Here are several typical scenarios, each with its own considerations and steps to take for a successful entry.

Scenario A: Everyone wants help

If all parties to the conflict ask for your help, whether you are inside or outside an organization, your work in the entry phase is easier. You still need to generate credibility, select a conflict approach to assure a sense of safety for all the participants and outline your expectations. But you begin with fewer initial barriers.

Scenario B: One party asks for intervention

If one of the parties asks you to intervene, your initial job is to hear the person out and then approach the other party. To return to the first example in this chapter, Larry might say, "John, thanks for telling me what you see happening and how frustrating it is. I'll talk to Sam and see if he is willing to explore a solution with us." When Larry sees Sam, it is important for him to acknowledge the tentative nature of his information. He might begin by saying, "Sam, John chatted briefly with me about some struggles the two of you are having. I might be able to be of some help to both of you. Would you consider sitting down together so we can make certain our meeting with the CEO goes smoothly?"

Scenario C: The manager is the mediator

Because managers often regulate conflict by arbitration or by edict, when you are the manager of people you think should be in mediation, you need to set the stage carefully. If you have typically managed disputes more traditionally prior to this time, you will need to explain why you want this conflict handled by mediation, explain your view of the mediation process, and, most importantly, explain your role and your stake in the outcome.

If you have two project managers who cannot work together well enough to complete a project, you might begin addressing the situation this way:

"Telling each of you that you must cooperate and produce has not worked. You are both stymied and I am frustrated, which tells me that what we've been doing is not working. I would like each of you to discuss what you need to be successful, especially from each other, as well as what you need from me. I will listen and help you hear each other out. Whatever you decide — as long as it supports our product release date and honors the need to have both your teams cooperate — I will support you. I value your contributions and want to give both of you as much latitude and support as possible. If there are issues that arise as we talk that I think will violate some important parameters of the project, I will let you know. I know this is a different process, but what we have been doing, I think you will agree, has not worked. Continuing the same way we have been puts us all in a precarious position regarding our credibility and future flexibility with projects."

Because this is a new process, initial attempts at problem solving with mediation may well take longer than simply issuing a managerial mandate. But you will find that the agreements reached for this particular conflict are more likely to endure and also will be more likely to prevent later eruptions.

Scenario D: Acting at a secondary party's request

Another scenario is when someone who is a secondary party to the dispute asks you to intervene: a boss who insists that conflicts must be settled so work can proceed. A manager two or three levels above the conflict could demand an end to complaints about a certain procedure or product. A Board of Directors could mandate that certain productivity standards be met within a given time frame.

In such conditions, your job as mediator is even more delicate. You need to:

Know and communicate to the participants the set of circumstances.

For example: "I understand the Board President has asked you both to be here and that you may feel some undue pressure from his being involved. He felt this approach was preferable to forcing you to comply with his decision. What he asks is that you come up with a plan by next week that involves both functional teams, that costs no more than X dollars, and that stops the open hostility being expressed between both teams."

Acknowledge the negative and positive aspects of the situation.

For example: "I know this may be frustrating, but I think you will have a great deal more credibility for using this process than if you were simply obeying orders from higher up. You still are in charge of most of the decisions made here."

Indicate what is at stake for the person requesting the mediation and what is at stake for the participants.

For example: "The Director is accountable to the Vice President on this issue and must have a decision before his meeting with the V.P. This project is a central part of the Director's objectives this year. If we get this settled, the Director will know you supported him, you will build credibility and are likely to be given more freedom in the next project."

Indicate at the outset how both parties will be protected in the process.

For example: "Agreements the two of you make will be communicated upward, but the details of the dispute will not. There may be other conditions you want to set so that you can explore issues in as much depth as you need without feeling like you are airing your dirty laundry in front of the Vice President."

If the parties deny that problems exist, you will need to be a bit confrontive at this stage.

If the people pressing for resolution are those in lower power positions, the mediator needs to protect their identities while acknowledging their stake in the conflict and its outcome. For example: "A lot of people working under both of you are concerned about the negative work environment and find it hard to concentrate on their tasks. If the quality of your work and history of your good working relationships are to continue, we need to resolve this conflict."

In any scenario, it is better to frame the mediation in terms of the positive benefit to the participants if they agree to mediate rather than threatening with negative consequences if they do not resolve the conflict. Sometimes bringing them to the table may require reminding them of the consequences of non-agreement, but the focus should be on the gains. People tend to operate in good faith when they know they will benefit from the final results.

Generating Credibility

As you begin the entry stage of mediation, it is essential to enhance the participants' sense of trust and safety. One element that helps to build trust is credibility — organizational, personal and procedural credibility. Let us look at these aspects in some detail.

Organizational credibility is enhanced when the mediator is of equal or higher position than the disputants. Just as a child in a family cannot effectively intervene in a parental dispute, the number two person in Research and Development normally cannot expect to succeed when intervening between two R&D vice presidents. Within an organization, the mediator needs to be a trusted person of equal or higher status in another department or someone with a designated role that lends credibility to the mediation, like a representative from Human Resources or Employee Relations.

Some organizations are experimenting with having a cadre of trained mediators designated to handle disputes, but they are struggling with the difficulties of conducting successful mediations across organizational levels and lines.

If you are the manager of those in conflict, you build credibility by telling the truth about your own stake in the conflict. For example, "I am bothered by people going at one another and I want to help get a smoother work environment."

You develop **Personal credibility** by the qualities you demonstrate as you mediate. Taking sides is the antithesis of effective mediation, however covert or subtle you believe you may be. Deciding who is right guarantees the ultimate failure of a mediation. Above all else, a mediator needs to be a *compassionate truth teller*, able to help the participants clearly see what is happening without any hostility for either party.

Among the specific qualities that emerge repeatedly in mediation research is flexibility of style. You need to be highly empathic as well as a vigorous salesperson when needed by the participants. You also need to be persistent and patient, conveying the sense that you will be there with the disputants through the whole process and that you are hopeful that a beneficial agreement can be reached. Often you need to be unobtrusive, guiding the process and letting the participants take credit for their success. Your role is not that of the rescuer, the savior or the hero of the hour, even if the disputants try to attribute an agreement to your skills. Re-focusing the attention back on their hard work, persistence, and goodwill helps the disputants continue to own their stake in the process.

To be a successful mediator, you also need *control over your feelings*. This does not mean that you are not to have any feelings or that you can't express any feelings during a mediation. You can use your own emotions productively by saying how concerned you are about the state of affairs, how sad you are about the resentments and hurts that people have endured or how glad and hopeful you are to see the parties working cooperatively and reducing their stress.

Often when the mediator expresses emotion for the benefit of both parties, it helps unfreeze the hearts of people locked in conflict and allows them to express deeper concerns. Stone walls don't have the warmth to create safety. Comments such as "That must make you sad when you are not getting recognized;" "I would be mad if I had to miss an important family event because of a work commitment;" "I know it must be difficult to feel as if you have little power here" can help to soften the dispute.

But, control of your feelings *does* mean doing your best to stay impartial. If you begin to assign blame to one disputant and side with another, you are no longer mediating but have become a party to the conflict. Knowing your emotions, quickly correcting yourself if you begin to take sides and re-directing your focus to the good of both parties are key parts of controlling your emotions.

Just as you train for a marathon, you can train for mediation, practicing good communication skills daily before you mediate disputes so you have a base for effective action. The ability to quickly diagnose a conflict and to understand the underlying issues before (or along with) those involved in the dispute also add to your credibility. You can improve your diagnostic skills by becoming more aware of your own interests in conflicts. You also can focus on improving your listening skills. Consistently paraphrasing others with whom you work helps toward clarifying your understanding.

Finally, *a sense of humor* can be a valuable asset during tense times. Gentle good humor provides a brief break in the tension and gives people a chance to distance from their role in a dispute.

Awash in accusations about a group's malicious motives, one mediator said that if the parties could bring as much creativity to resolving the dispute as they expended in creating and elaborating stories about the other group's intentions, the problem would be solved. Humor needs to be well timed and introduced only after rapport has been built between mediator and disputants.

Your demeanor is the most potent element you bring to the mediation process. It can work for you or against you. If you are angry and frustrated, those emotions will "leak out" during your attempts to help others. On the other hand, if you are self-aware and have developed your soft and hard sides, you can use all these personal qualities effectively and make your mediation work successful. In sum, you build personal credibility by all your actions.

Procedural Credibility is built by explaining the mediation process and dealing with the expectations of the parties in conflict. You may specify the steps to be followed — for example, interviewing both parties, then convening them for negotiation. You also clarify some *outcomes* they can expect, such as putting an agreement in written form.

Participants in an ongoing struggle are usually unclear and misinformed abut how mediation works. Some may think it involves holding formal hearings and deciding the case much like a judge or an arbitrator. Others may see mediators merely as ineffective listeners who have little impact. Introducing the process is often a good beginning that helps build credibility. For example: "Sometimes people are unsure of what mediation is. Basically, it involves making sure you are both treated with respect, that you both get an equal chance to talk and then developing some creative solutions to the conflict."

Asking "What is your image of how mediation can play a role in this conflict?" or "What impressions do you have about how mediation works?" provides a way of checking on participants' expectations. You need to make it clear that you are not "fixing" the problem but rather that, as mediator, your role is to help them resolve their difficulties. Their willingness to talk to you about the process can be cited as a good sign that they can work out their problems.

Mediation requires your acting in an impartial way. You may need to explain that, although you will not take sides, you may need to talk to the people separately as well as jointly to work on the issues.

In addition, you need to assure them of *confidentiality*. Normally, you may say, "Everything you say to me I will keep confidential.

Later, you may choose to tell another person, but it will be your choice, your decision and not mine." If for any reason there are limits to the confidentiality, the limits need to be clearly stated at the outset.

Throughout the process, you *infuse optimism* — not with a false display of cheerfulness, but saying, for example, "It looks difficult at this point, but working through problems such as these is often not as hard as it looks at the beginning. First, we have to get the two of you in conversation with one another."

Last, you *solicit any reservations* they may have about the process. Participants often worry about confidentiality, what the negative consequences might be and whether or not you are siding with the other party. If the process does not seem appropriate to all the parties involved, this is the time to get any reservations out in the open, to create the sense of safety they need and to modify the process so that it will work for them.

Selecting a Conflict Approach that Fits the Problem at Hand

One important task of entry is to discover whether or not mediation is appropriate for the particular problem at hand. Sometimes a conflict might best be handled some other way — with a mandate from a manager or through a group discussion that forms the basis for a managerial decision.

Return to the stages of conflict shown in the Struggle Spectrum, page 18, when deciding whether or not to proceed with a mediation.

The Stuggle Spectrum can also serve as a guide for finding ways to contain a dispute that may be escalating. For instance, with an upcoming contract negotiation, a labor union may begin making noises that may sound like a Stage 4 campaign. By looking at conditions that keep a conflict at Stages 2 and 3, a company leader could decide to respond in ways that would keep the situation from worsening. Instituting discussions, negotiations or joint decision-making would help to create conditions to make negotiations more productive for both sides.

To determine whether or not mediation is appropriate, consider the following questions:

What is the history of the conflict?

Negative history between people can be dealt with. Yet, when people do not agree about past events, they are often unable to move forward and deal successfully with current problems. It is important for a mediator to acknowledge that, more than likely, the participants will always have different perceptions of past events — that is partly why there is a conflict. But agreeing on the past isn't necessary in order to move forward. In fact, they must decide the extent to which they want the past to control their futures. Having acknowledged that they have something at stake and stand to gain or lose something if they fail to reach an agreement, they may be more willing to proceed to solve current problems. Presenting these kinds of ideas helps the parties re-frame the dispute so that they are willing to move forward.

When the hurts run very deep, it may also be important to suggest that the participants heal the old wounds. Perhaps in individual caucuses, you can suggest steps for letting go of past hurts and helping both to recognize and to experience the grieving process.

Typically, grieving is a process of moving through a series of stages: denial, anger, bargaining, sadness, depression and, finally, acceptance. Providing information about the stages of the grieving process may help the parties identify the phase they are in. A more subtle approach is for the mediator to identify the stage of grieving each of the parties has reached and then respond in a way that helps them move through that stage.[1] Responding in ways that help those who are grieving to let go of old wounds, hurts and losses also helps everyone to move toward acceptance.

Another option is to have each make a list of the other's transgressions, noting which are forgivable and which ones they consider unforgivable. The next step is to ask if there is anything the other party can do to move the "unforgivables" to the forgivable side of their ledger. Sometimes a simple apology or an acknowledgement that there was hurt can be sufficient. These can become requests for action during the mediation process.

For any issues left on the unforgivable side, ask whether the person is willing to let go by acknowledging the pain that has been caused and to work to prevent future hurts. While this may take some time and coaching, the person in conflict needs to make a conscious decision about what to do with a hurtful history. Making this decision consciously often prevents later unconscious sabotage of agreements that are made.

Although a hostile history by itself need not be a barrier to mediation, if one or both parties has revenge as a primary goal, mediation may not be the answer. Arbitration — in the form of a managerial decision or litigation — may be the way to go. You must decide about the most constructive approach, given the circumstances of the conflict.

Who are the stakeholders?

You must identify *all* those who have a vested interest in any outcome to the conflict, regardless of their level in the organization. If, for example, you are not the manager of the disputants, their boss(es) may need to be notified of the mediation, asked for permission to mediate, and/or asked about conditions that will affect the agreement.

Sometimes stakeholders remain hidden until mediation begins. Ironically, these hidden stakeholders are often the people whose interests are served by continuing negative conflicts. In one situation, the Finance Director kept control of the situation by fueling the fires of conflict between two of his subordinates. As long as they were fighting, the Finance Director could appear to play the comfortable role of "benevolent father." Whenever the subordinates clarified their needs and perceptions, the Finance Director moved in and rekindled the fire. Finally, the CEO had to be prevailed upon to bring the Finance Director to the table and clarify *his* interests.

Be alert to the possibility that stakeholders may emerge during the process. You will need to include them in your work.

It is important to remember that conflict often arises as a result of a system, not from individual behavior. Consequently, the bosses may need to hear some feedback from the mediator on how their behavior may support dysfunctional conflicts and ways they can begin to reinforce more constructive behavior.

What is the actual (and the desired) relationship between the parties?

Oftentimes, people in conflict may have had a good working relationship in the past and wish to recapture it, if they can manage this dispute. Reminding them of a positive history can sometimes be enough to re-focus the conflict positively. Some people and some organizations place a high value on quality relationships, a value that can be evoked to help the participants re-focus. For example: "I know people are valued in this organization. That value supports this method," or "I have heard that having a strong community is important to you."

On the other hand, hostility may be so high that mediation is not the best method for managing the conflict. Or if there is little desire to establish a working relationship, the interdependence between the parties may not be strong enough to warrant mediation. In that case, other methods of conflict management — such as a managerial decision — may be required.

How are the parties interdependent?

To have a constructive conflict, the people involved must see how they can affect each other and understand that they need something from each other. A reminder of this two-way relationship may be necessary at this stage. For example, you might say, "I know that you each need the skills of the other to complete this project. With cooperation, you both stand to gain. If not, I assume you both will lose credibility with management when you can't meet the product release date."

If, however, there is little interdependence, and the parties can get most of what they want without going through the time-consuming process of a mediation, you may need to suggest other conflict management routes. Consider the example of one city manager who wanted to build his team of department directors by having them discuss and resolve virtually all conflicts as a team, even though many of the issues that arose did not affect the other team members. In fact, the frequent meetings were the *source* of conflict. One-on-one meetings between the city manager and directors with issues that did not depend on other departments was the preferred solution. Mediation was not appropriate.

What is the balance of power between the parties?

To have a constructive conflict, the people involved need to have nearly equal perceived power. This is not to say that they must have equal positions in the organization, but rather that they have a similar amount of influence on one another, in terms of their overlapping goals. For example, when one person is a manager who controls resources and information and the other has a special expertise needed for the group's success, they both have important currencies in the dispute. To remind them of their mutual influence and to keep both parties honest and engaged, the mediator might remind them that, although there is a difference in their positions, both know they each can affect the other.

The mediator may also need to help balance the power by setting ground rules to protect a lower-power person in the conflict. Male/female disputes are a good example. In an organizational setting, the woman often has less power — especially if she is the only woman on a work team. The mediator can draw on a number of techniques to balance the power and protect both parties. These could include:

- ▸ Insisting on confidentiality, so the woman is not singled out as "the bitch" by colleagues nor is the man labeled "weak" for "giving in."

▸ Enlisting the support from powerful people in the organization who support equal treatment and believe in creating a positive working environment.

▸ Framing the conflict so that the results can be described in terms of the strength and courage it takes to solve problems in-depth rather than go for a quick fix.

▸ If the more powerful person in the conflict refuses to operate in good faith, a last resort is to remind disputants of the legal consequences of non-agreement. Such threats, however veiled, should be used cautiously. Used prematurely or too aggressively, they can derail the proceedings.

It is important, however, not to overcorrect the balance either — which may involve a bit of self-examination about your attitudes about power. If you naturally tend to side with the underdog, for example, you may unconsciously tip the scale in a conflict. By evoking fear in the party with the higher power, you could unintentionally rigidify that party's response to the conflict.

The issue of power balancing is so important that we have devoted an entire section to its ramifications. See Chapter 6, Managing the Power Arena.

What preferences do the disputants have for controlling the outcome versus having someone mandate an answer?

One of the reasons mediation is empowering is that the participants retain more control of the solutions and their implementation. While this appeals to most people, others may not want accountability or visibility. In some circumstances people may feel unable to make as well-informed a choice as their manager, for example. If these desires are strong enough, mediation may not be the best choice.

What preferences are there for "going public" with the dispute and its solution?

Sometimes an issue is so important that a person or group *wants* the dialogue to be public, perhaps to build support or gain power.

This can often be the situation in environmental disputes or in matters that affect public safety. If this is the case, including more people in the mediation may satisfy the need for openness. Or, mediation may not be the appropriate method if you find that the desire for public disclosure outweighs the need to resolve the dispute.

What organizational norms support (or block) mediation?

If an organization is extremely "conflict averse," then protecting the privacy of the disputants will be crucial during and after the mediation. Mediation may, in fact, need to be framed as a peaceful means of problem solving so that the word "conflict" is not mentioned. We found a striking example when conducting a program called "Constructive Conflict" for a conference outside the United States. Upon arriving, we found the program listed our presentation as "Everyday Problem Solving for Ladies and Gentlemen." The title change provided an unmistakable clue to the group's conflict norms, showing that the topic had to be approached with the proverbial kid gloves.

On the other hand, if the organization requesting mediation has a reputation for innovation, the process can be cast as "an innovative approach to managing conflict."

What are the expectations of the disputants?

The parties may be in such pain that they grasp at mediation as some sort of magic panacea. Educating about mediation as you build procedural credibility will help make their expectations more realistic. On the other hand, when tensions run so high that the parties think nothing will work, you may need to explain that very difficult conflicts have been managed with mediation, perhaps citing examples from within their organization or highly visible international conflicts. Reassure the participants and let them know you have hope for this conflict if those involved are willing to operate in good faith.

Clarify which expectations are realistic, in terms of what can actually be accomplished, at the same time affirming that after mediation, hard work and monitoring will be required to support the agreements.

While mediation is not magic, it has the capacity to turn destructive communication into positive, life-enhancing energy.

Addressing all these conditions during the entry takes time, but experience shows that it helps the mediation flow smoothly and allows the parties to be realistic, hopeful and protected.

Indicating Your Expectations for a Successful Mediation

Establishing the conditions for effective mediation requires making direct requests of the participants. This creates a workable situation for the mediator, allows you to model being direct and begins to build clear relationships in which constructive conflict can flourish.

This list of expectations will give you a sense of the conditions to be specified at the entry phase.

Begin to define the ground rules

Disputants will want to tell you their story of the conflict in the entry phase, especially when there is urgency and/or open hostility. Though you will want to curtail a lengthy description of the conflict until you have agreement from all parties that they will commit to the mediation process, it's important to listen to some of the story so the participants feel heard and so you have some idea of the conflict dynamics. You need to begin setting communication ground rules in this stage, and expand on them later as you begin negotiations. You likely will need to say that you will listen to both sides, that you expect no interruptions while the other is talking, that you will tolerate no name-calling and blaming and that you are here to work for all parties, to protect their interests and needs. To do so, you will need for them to communicate in ways that you and the others can hear and understand. If the mediation moves quickly from entry to diagnosis and negotiation in the first session, you will need to set more thorough ground rules with the help of participants. A full coverage of ground rules is given in Chapter 3.

Estimate the time needed

Some people demand to know how long the process is going to take. Be realistic about the minimum time that could be involved and, when you can provide a range of time, do so. But sometimes all you can say is that the process is shorter when people operate in good faith and cooperate with each other, or simply, "The amount of time will pretty much depend on you."

Specify when you will meet and with whom

All meetings involving specified people should be spelled out clearly to reduce suspicion. Sometimes, in order to get a clear understanding of the issues, a mediator may call separate meetings with people or announce a board meeting that only some members can attend. All parties in a dispute should be notified of these meetings and their purposes and a plan should be developed for including others whose voices need to be heard. "Harmless" meetings often turn into symbols of why others cannot be trusted — even a previously respected leader.

Insure the accessibility of the disputants

Sometimes in a conflict, people who are nervous or angry respond by being inaccessible by phone or by "forgetting" meetings. You must spell out what you need from them, including being on time for meetings and having the parties return your phone calls within a certain time.

Detail the kinds of information or people to which you need access

If a conflict is complex and will take more than a few hours, you may need personnel records, past memos or discussions with others in the organization to get a realistic perspective of the conflict and its impact. Let the disputants know your need for information and also how you will save face for them if you have to talk to others. For example, you might say, "As you know, I will be reviewing past personnel records to get a clear idea of the history of the conflict. I have told people in personnel that both of you are very interested in reaching a mutual agreement and will appreciate their assistance. They have also agreed not to discuss the issue with anyone else, except to reiterate that both of you want to reach agreement."

Set limits on their behavior

During a conflict, people can take actions that, consciously or not, may escalate the conflict. These may include venting their feelings by gossiping with others, forming coalitions to build their power base, talking with the media to explain their side or going to people higher in the organization to seek protection. It's helpful to reach an agreement with those in conflict about what kinds of behavior will or won't be tolerated, to keep from making the mediation difficult or impossible. These agreements should be framed to show how adhering to limits on their behavior will serve each party's interests and how violations will harm them.

In one public policy dispute, all parties agreed to issue the same statement to the media: "We are working hard toward an agreement to benefit all parties." Prior media reports had served to fuel the differences and inflame the conflict, so this unified front served everyone's interest by containing the information until an agreement was reached.

Determine who will be informed of the results and how that will be done

It is critical that the participants know who will be informed about the mediation and how they will be told. You could decide that the actual agreement will need to be sent to their boss or to the manager, but that the specifics of the dialogue — who said what to whom — will not be reported. Often at the end of the mediation, the parties create a "press release" for those in the organization who want to know how it went.

Specify the consequences if the parties do not cooperate

Occasionally, one party may refuse to cooperate, acting as if the conflict is entirely the other's problem. This needs to be confronted gently by saying something like, "Am I correct in assuming that you do not want to proceed with the dialogue and are willing to risk the consequences of product delay and lowered credibility?" Your task is simply to verbalize what is at risk, mirroring what the participants have told you they stand to gain or lose, and to do so without any hostility.

Entry steps can be accomplished quickly or they may take considerable time, depending on the dispute and the participants' perception of you and your role. Building a solid and safe container of agreements, procedures and considerations makes it possible for people to engage in the often difficult task of coming to common agreement. When that container can be successfully constructed, even the most heated conflict has a chance of being transformed. Without it, even an apparently simple issue can turn into a hopeless impasse. This safety net is what you, as mediator, and the disputing parties must rely on whenever a snag is hit.

APPLICATION

► The **Entry Checklist** guides you through what needs to be accomplished at the first stage of mediation.

► A **Sample Memo** shows how to set the stage for a successful mediation.

► A **Sample Entry Dialogue** is presented to give a feel for how a mediator combines the skills, roles and methods of the entry stage to build rapport with the participants and confidence in the mediation process.

YARBROUGH
GROUP

Entry Checklist

Entry should accomplish

1. Greater confidence in the process and the mediator

2. Commitment to follow-through

3. Greater trust in a successful outcome

As you plan, proceed with, or reflect on the entry, have you

☐ Obtained information on conditions for mediation? How did this situation come about? Who has what stakes in the process? Who will be told about the outcome?

☐ Built organizational, personal, procedural credibility? Considered if you have the position to mediate? Reminded yourself of the qualities of a good mediator?

☐ Explained the mediation process?

☐ Explained mediation: your role, process to be used, confidentiality, private meetings?

☐ Considered different conflict approaches? What else could the disputants do to solve the problem, with what consequences?

☐ Made clear your expectations as to time, information, consequences, conditions for the mediation and behaviors required?

☐ Asked about any reservations and, from those, built in as much safety as possible?

☐ Obtained an actual statement from all disputants that they are ready to work on a mutual agreement?

YARBROUGH
GROUP

Sample Memo

July 24
To: Conflict Participants
From: Elaine Yarbrough
Re: Mediation for XYZ Group

I spoke with Shelly yesterday about beginning work with you to increase mutual cooperation and to reduce the stress on everyone. She and Frank filled me in on some of the history of your group, especially some of the strains since the reorganization. Shelly indicates that each of you is ready and willing to look at what you need individually and as a group and to work towards meeting those needs in ways that your agreements are kept long term.

I told Shelly that I would do the following:

1. Interview each of you individually to get an understanding of each person's perspective and needs. This would include interviewing your manager who is central to these issues and will be important in supporting people in the long run. August 17 is the day I need to do the interviews. If there is a problem with this date, Shelly will let me know.

2. After the interviews, decide if I think there is sufficient commitment to reaching mutual agreements and sticking to them.

3. If so, convene the group August 27 and the afternoon of August 28 to explore the issues, reach some critical agreements and establish ways to support, reinforce and monitor those agreements after the

meeting so that they will endure. Based on the issues, we may need more time, but we can decide that on the 28th.

Here is what I need from you:

1. A commitment to working in good faith on these issues for the short and long term.

2. A commitment of time on August 17, 27, 28 — and perhaps other days if necessary to reach stable, workable agreements. The amount of time this takes will pretty much depend on you.

3. Accessibility to me and to each other. That is, returning phone calls and providing the information necessary to clearly identify needs, so we can meet them.

4. An examination of your own as well as others' actions to understand how this conflict keeps perpetuating itself.

5. A willingness to work on the present issues and move forward, even though there is a great deal of history that supports the current patterns. This does not mean we will not discuss and examine the history, but we can actually solve only the current problems and work to make the future brighter.

All indications seem to show you are ready to move forward and I am eager to work with you. I know, if all are committed, you can turn this situation around and create a more satisfying working situation and a more productive team.

Sample Entry Dialogue

This conversation demonstrates how to build rapport and confidence during the entry process.

The context: Two parties in a small, non-profit community organization are involved in a dispute. Lydia, who has an eighth-grade education, has been in charge of cleaning and upkeep for the organization for thirty years. A new executive director of the organization, Fred, has come from the East coast. The organization operates with a Board of Directors and the Board President has asked the mediator to work with Fred and Lydia. Talking with each briefly on the phone, the mediator has arranged to meet with Lydia and Fred in a neutral place, a meeting room in the agency.

Mediator: *I appreciate your coming, I know this is difficult. But I want to get to know you. Lydia, I've known your name but I haven't met you. I'm Elaine Yarbrough.*

Lydia: I'm Lydia.

Mediator: *Very nice to meet you. I know how highly you are thought of here. Fred, I know that you come highly recommended to this position and people are very excited about your being here, so I would like to welcome you.*

Fred: Last things best.

Mediator: *So, Fred, you've been here about two months now?*

Fred: Yes — two or two and a half.

Mediator: *Since I have been in this community for a long time and know people here, I know that you're highly valued and that people are very excited about your joining this organization. I personally want this session to work and want to talk to both of you about how it will operate. Could either of you tell me why you think you're here?*

Fred: You mean in this room? Or in this organization?

Mediator: *In this particular room, meeting here with me. I know this wouldn't be your favorite thing, of all possible things you could list, but how do you think you got here?*

Fred: Well, I'm here because I can't get Lydia to cooperate. She's talking behind my back, causing all kinds of problems. I'm trying to turn this organization around and she's really putting a monkey wrench in all that. That's why I'm here. I just want you to get her on board.

Mediator: *Okay. So, it's worth your time to work it out because you want to succeed?*

Fred: Oh yes.

Mediator: *Okay. And Lydia, why do you think you're here?*

Lydia: Because they're trying to do something to me here. I've worked with this company for thirty years and they're trying to take my livelihood away. I don't know what he is trying to do. He just came in here. I've been here thirty years and and he's trying to take my money away from me and hurt my family and . . .

Mediator: *So, it sounds like you're pretty nervous about what's going on.*

Lydia: Well, what can I do? I'm not educated. I don't have anything else — and he's going to do what he wants to do.

Mediator: *It sounds like you are really committed to this place.*

Lydia: Yes.

Mediator: *You've served here a long time?*

Lydia: Yes, this is my home, this is where I work. I've been here thirty years and this is my family — until he comes in.

Mediator: *So, it sounds like you have a lot of investment in working and supporting Fred, working with him, so that you also get what you need.*

Lydia: I want to protect my position. This is my position. This is my life. I have to support my family.

Mediator: *You don't want to leave here and you want to be well reimbursed for what you do?*

Lydia: Absolutely.

Mediator: *So that's a key issue for you?*

Lydia: Yes, I don't want my position taken away. I need to feed my family. I need to be here.

Mediator: *Okay. So both of you have pretty important stakes for being here. And both of you also know that Sally, the Board President, asked me to be here. I told her that I would meet with you initially, but that it has to be okay with both of you for us to proceed with this. I need to tell you that she has a high stake in this outcome. Do you understand that?*

Fred: Sure, I'm alright with that. I've had a long talk with her.

Mediator: *Okay. And, Lydia, you've known Sally for a long time. You under-stand her investment in keeping you, a valued employee? She was, of course, in charge of hiring you, Fred, so she also has an investment in you, too.*

Lydia: So, you three aren't in on this together? You and Sally and Fred?

Mediator: *No. Was that one of your worries?*

Lydia: Well, yes. I mean, you're all educated and professional people and I can't fight you. I worry about how I am going to protect myself.

Mediator: *Well, that's one of my jobs, actually. You don't know me very well, but you do know Sally.*

Lydia: Yes, and I like Sally.

Mediator: *Yes. And maybe I just ought to check this out, because I did just assume it. Do you assume Sally thinks you're a valued person and wants to keep you?*

Lydia: I don't know. Since Fred's been here, I don't know. Maybe he's put some ideas in her head.

Mediator: *So that's not really settled for you, is it?*

Lydia: No, not really.

Mediator: *Okay, let me tell you what I know and then I really do want you to say if you believe it.*

Lydia: Okay.

Mediator: *Okay. Sally has told me directly how much she values you. All the evidence of the past thirty years would suggest that: your promotions, your ability to make decisions. You've grown increasingly more able to make actual decisions in your area. So none of the data would tell me she doesn't value you.*

Lydia: Sally's always been my friend.

Mediator: *Yes, and I know that you value her.*

Lydia: Yes.

Mediator: *On the other hand, she really values Fred, so we're not trying to decide who's good and bad here, you understand. Fred comes highly recommended, too, so Sally's good faith efforts are with both of you. And my job — perhaps I ought to say what my job is. My job is to come in, not with a solution on how you ought to work this out, but to find ways for both of you to get what you need out of this. We'll know more of what each of you needs* *as we go on, but, Fred, for you to feel like an integral part of this organization, to have your people there for you so you can succeed. For you, Lydia, to keep your position and to be valued and to be compensated. My job is to protect those interests for both of you.*

Fred: Well, unfortunately those are at odds.

Mediator: *They might look like it now.*

Fred: Well, I've tried to institute some of the best management practices. I went to Princeton. And she just resists the whole thing. It's clear that we need to go from hourly wages to salaried employees so that we can contain costs. It's always a problem in an organization like this.

Mediator: *So, containing costs is one of your big objectives.*

Fred: Yes, that's right. And to bring in some of these management practices. I mean, I went to school for six months to learn this program, and when I come in here, all I get is resistance from people.

Mediator: *Okay.*

Fred: I mean, it's been demonstrated clear across the country that this is the way to run organizations — and I can't get people to cooperate.

Lydia: He doesn't understand . . .

Mediator: *Well, we'll work on that. But your goal is clearly to succeed here.*

Fred: Yes. And to bring some some good management practices into this organization.

Mediator: *Yes, they help you to succeed.*

Fred: Yes, it's about time.

Mediator: *It's not clear yet just how we'll work all this out. But my role is to protect your being a valued person and being compensated, perhaps not in the way that you were in the past, or maybe not even in the way you have suggested. It may be something else that we dream up. But so that you're a valued employee, Lydia, and so that you can succeed, Fred. I don't see those as mutually exclusive. If we can hang in here long enough we might be able to see that.*

Fred: Well, I hope so.

Mediator: *Another role of mine is to listen to both of you carefully, to give you both some protection. So, Fred, we're certainly not going to take this out of here and do a media interview about Fred being in trouble. We're not* *going to have the word out in the organization so that Lydia feels put down. We're going to keep this in here, contained. The only thing Sally wants us to report to her is the decision we make.*

Fred: So, what we say will be confidential?

Mediator: *Absolutely. I won't spread it and I need an agreement from you that you won't spread it.*

Lydia: And, you won't side with him? He's more educated and has more persuasion skills. You know, I can only tell the truth.

Mediator: *Well, Fred will, too, although it may be a different truth. And, no, I won't side with him. And if you think I'm siding with somebody — and I'll offer this to you, Fred, too, — you need to call me on that.*
    Is there another assurance you need? I know this is important.

Lydia: I don't want him . . . I mean, he just said that he was bringing in good management practices, as if I weren't a good manager for thirty years.

Mediator: *You have such a sense of the whole organization. You know all the things that are running well — and all the things that people have been belly-aching about for years, so I know you're not saying some things don't need to be improved.*

Lydia: That's true.

Mediator: *In fact, with your background, you have invaluable information for Fred.*

Lydia: If he would listen to me.

Mediator: *Yes. And, Fred, you know from those valuable management practices that you've got to get information from your people.*

Fred: Right. But if she'll stop blocking me, we'll do something.

Mediator: *So, it sounds like we need to have agreements both ways. If you want to use her skills, you'll have to do some things. And if you want to use his skills, you'll have to do some things. Does that sound fair?*

Lydia: As as long as he's not out to get me and to get me fired.

Mediator: *Okay. Maybe I ought to check on that right now, because this keeps coming up.*

Lydia: Okay.

Mediator: *What can you say about that, Fred? Can you reassure her?*

Fred: Yes. It doesn't have anything to do with her personally. I just want to bring the best management practices into this organization and when I try to do that, then someone like Lydia runs off and says, "You're out to fire me." I'm not out to fire them, I'm out to contain costs. And then she took it as a personal vendetta.

Mediator: *Okay. Then, can you tell Lydia directly that this is not leading to her personal firing?*

Fred: Yes, Lydia, I'm not going to fire you. I don't want to fire you. That would be dumb. Our members of the Board think you're the most valuable person in this organization, next to me.

Lydia: Well, that's probably true.

Fred: So, I'm not going to fire you. But I try to make a change and all I get is resistance.

Mediator: *So, do you see where you may be able to use Lydia's background? And, Lydia, I think what Fred is asking of you is that he'd like you to be open to some of his ideas, too. It seems like a fair exchange. Is it?*

Lydia: As long as he's not going to use them against me, I'll be open.

Mediator: *Okay. From what he just said, can we believe it enough to proceed, do you think?*

Lydia: I think so.

Mediator: *Okay. If that comes up again, please let me know.*

Lydia: Okay.

Fred: And it's really important to me that, when I talk about issues, that I could talk about them without Lydia always taking it personally and thinking that I'm trying to push her out or starve her to death or something. That's not what I'm after.

Mediator: *There may need to be some reassurance around that?*

Fred: You mean me to her?

Mediator: *Yes, I mean like we just did. Because there may be times that you need some reassurance from Lydia that she won't take what we say and go out and tattle.*

Fred: Yes, that's true.

Mediator: *That seems a fair exchange. So do I have your agreement that what gets said in here is confidential only to the three of us?*

Fred: Yes.

Mediator: *Okay. And, Lydia?*

Lydia: I was just trying to protect myself and tell my friends so they would protect me, too, but I will do that.

Fred: Now, this means the Board President. This means that if I say something you don't like, you won't go tell her that?

Lydia: I won't go tell Sally. Okay. If I can trust you, then I will try it.

Mediator: *Okay. And if those issues come back up, even as we're getting on with this, you need to let me know and I will guarantee to both of you that we will stop and do what we need to do. Is that okay?*

Lydia: Okay.

Fred: Okay.

Mediator: *There may be times — and in light of my telling you what my role is, I want you to get clear on this — there may be times that I will want to talk to each of you individually. During those times, I won't be making a deal with either of you. I'll be trying to get clarity on what you each want so that we can bring clear issues back to the meeting. Does that seem clear to you, about individual meetings?*

Fred: Yes, that's fine.

Mediator: *Okay. Any problem with that, Lydia?*

Lydia: Will you tell us if you are going to have individual meetings?

Mediator: *Yes, absolutely.*

Lydia: Okay.

Mediator: *Yes. In fact, I'll probably be doing it right here. Today I'll probably say, "Let's take a little break and, Lydia, I need to talk to you for ten minutes," and, "Fred, you can take a personal break and then I'll get back to you."*

Fred: So, we'd know right at the time?

Mediator: *Right. And if I'm going to talk to people individually over the phone, I will always let the other party know.*

Lydia: Okay.

Mediator: *Also, if you want to talk to me individually, you let me know.*

Fred: Okay.

Lydia: And you won't be going back and telling Sally what we're doing yet, until we agree?

Mediator: *No. I will keep my confidentiality. When Sally, or anybody else, asks me, I'll say "We're working on issues in good faith and we'll let you know when we have reached a decision."*

Fred: Do you take phone calls at home?

Mediator: *Not usually. If it is an absolute emergency I will. But I will give you the hours when you can reach me and, if that absolutely will not work, then you can call me at home. But I'll ask you to use that in good faith.*

Lydia: What does that mean?

Mediator: *That means that, unless it's an emergency, wait until the next day — because my home time is important to me. I have a young child and I try to protect that time. Is that fair enough?*

Fred: Yes.

Lydia: Yes.

Mediator: *Any questions about what we're doing?*

Fred: I'm concerned about Lydia living up to the agreements that we make.

Mediator: *When we get to them?*

Fred: Yes, because, the pattern from my perspective is that she goes behind closed doors and I'm kind of concerned about that. I mean, we can work this through and then Lydia goes, I'm not talking to you, I'm just doing my own thing. And if she does that, it's going to blow this whole thing up.

Mediator: *Lydia, this is important, because, just like you asked Fred for assurance that he's not out to fire you, it sounds like he needs assurance that you will play in good faith. Can you assure him of that?*

Lydia: Yes. The reason I talked to people was to protect myself against him, and if I know I'm protected here then I won't do that. But he has to live up to his agreement not to try to get me. I have a family to feed.

Fred: I've already said that's not what I'm trying to do.

Lydia: Okay.

Mediator: *So both of you have made assurances to each other. Can we believe them?*

Fred: I'm willing to try it.

Lydia: Me, too.

Mediator: *In a conflict, you're likely to read another's actions as signs that he or she has broken an agreement. So I would ask both of you that, if that comes up, and you think, "Oh, there goes Fred!" or, "Yep, there goes Lydia," that we come back together and you check out that perception before you make a decision to stop this process. Will you make an agreement with me on that?*

Fred: Sure.

Lydia: I will come to you first.

Mediator: *Okay. And if you don't, I need to tell you what my options are. I am believing both of you — that you're not out to fire her and that you're not out to do him in covertly. If either one of you breaks your agreement with me, then what I do is go to Sally and tell her that we have broken off, that you're not reaching agreement, and that probably the Board has to make a decision in this. Then, you two lose your choices.*

Lydia: I don't want that.

Fred: Yes. I don't think that would be wise, either. The Board would really muck it up.

Mediator: *Well, they are divided. You know that I would never do that unless you left me no choices and I don't see that as a likelihood.*

Fred: But you are saying it's contingent on us following our agreement.

Mediator: *That's right.*

Fred: Well, that's no problem for me.

Lydia: I'm an honest person.

Mediator: *Yes, you are and you know that. Any other reservations or concerns?*

Fred: How long will this take?

Mediator: *Quite frankly, I don't know.*

Fred: I thought you were the expert!

Mediator: *Only on the process. The timing will be pretty much contingent on how cooperative you are with each other. We'll meet for the four hours we agreed to and then we'll check on where we are. If we're done, we're done. If we're not done, we're not done.*

Fred: So, it's kind of up to us, is that what you're saying?

Mediator: *Yes. Of course I will be guiding you and maybe giving you a little nudge every now and then, because my expertise is around getting an agreement. But really, it's pretty much dependent upon you. Any problems with that?*

Fred: No, that's okay. I was kind of hoping you could say two-and-a-half hours.

Mediator: *No. We've got lots of things to do. What about you, Lydia? Do you have any problems with that?*

Lydia: Not with that. I'm just concerned that he has a higher position than me and, well, what he says will win out over what I say.

Mediator: *In here?*

Lydia: Yes.

Mediator: *Has that happened so far?*

Lydia: Not in here.

Mediator: *So the data we have in here indicates that is not happening.*

Lydia: No. I feel okay here.

Mediator: *I will assure you that it will continue to happen this way, that whatever information I get from Fred I'll also get your side of it.*

Lydia: So, I'm equal in here?

Mediator: *Yes, and let me just give you a little nudge, Lydia. Here's Fred, highly educated and comes from the East. But do you understand how much power you have in this organization?*

Lydia: No, ma'am.

Mediator: *Look me straight in the eye and say that. You know everybody in this organization and have for thirty years. You know everybody in the community, you've lived here fifty-five years. Fred's been here two months. So, you might not be able to step up to the podium and counter Fred. But it wouldn't take much for you to counter Fred. Fred knows that and you know it. So, do you want to fess up on that one?*

Lydia: Yes, I have a lot of friends..

Mediator: *And a lot of power. It's just a different power. Fred has a lot of power in his position and his background. He is valued. And you have a lot of networking.*

Fred: Yes. And I feel like I have no power at all with the staff.

Mediator: *See?*

Fred: The Board hires me and brings me in and I've got all these special schools and I tell everybody and nobody listens to me.

Mediator: *Isn't it interesting that both of you are feeling the same way? You're feeling that nobody will listen to you and you were brought in to do this work.*

Fred: Yes.

Mediator: *You're feeling like you're hanging out there to dry. Well, we might as well acknowledge that neither one of you feels very powerful. So how about we work on it?*

Lydia: I didn't know he felt that way.

Mediator: *Isn't that interesting?*
   Okay. I'll need your cooperation, I'll need your time. You've already committed to that. I'll need you to be as open with me as you can be and I'll be nudging you around that.

Fred: Would you like me to bring my secretary in to take notes on the meeting?

Mediator: *That's a very nice offer, but I think I'll do that.*

Fred: You mean you'll take notes yourself?

Mediator: *Yes, it helps me to keep thinking. Then I'll show you the notes.*

Fred: Wouldn't it be more efficient to bring my executive secretary in?

Mediator: *No, it would . . .*

Lydia: It compromises our confidentiality. It's risky.

Mediator: *It's risky.*

Fred: Oh.

Lydia: I don't want anybody else.

Fred: Well, I'm just trying to help the process.

Mediator: *I know you were and I appreciate that.*
   Let me just check in. You've agreed to do this, in this time frame, and to reach an agreement that serves you both. Are you willing to formally commit to this, to say, "Yes, I will do this in good faith."

Lydia: Yes, I will do this in good faith.

Mediator: *Okay. Good. How about you, Fred?*

Fred: I will, too. I'll do it in good faith.

Mediator: *Okay! Boy, I appreciate that — because I know how hard this is. I'm quite frankly tickled and have a lot of hope for this. I know how much you're both valued here.*

Fred: Well, I'm feeling a little better already. I mean, there's some tough stuff to go yet, but I feel a little better.

Lydia: Me, too.

Mediator: *Okay, then. I'll see you Tuesday at 2 p.m. Thank you very much.*

Lydia: Thank you.

Fred: Thanks very much. Sure you don't want me to bring my secretary in?

Mediator: *No, but thanks for the offer.*

Fred: Okay.

Mediator: *See you both on Tuesday.*

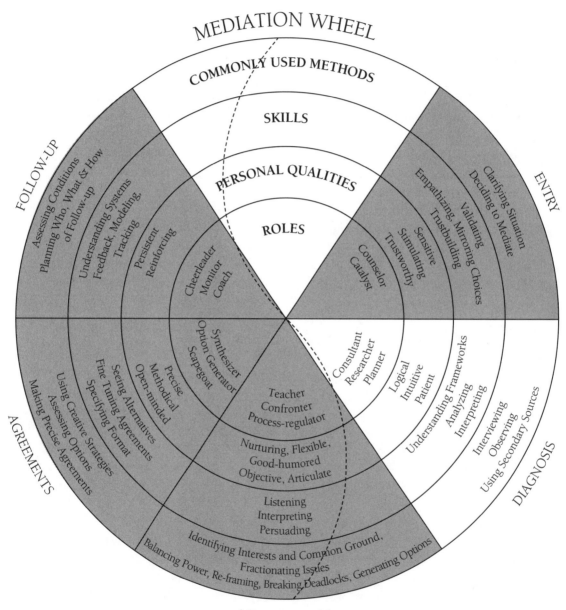

MEDIATION WHEEL

COMMONLY USED METHODS

SKILLS

PERSONAL QUALITIES

ROLES

FOLLOW-UP

Assessing Conditions
Planning Who, What & How
of Follow-up

Understanding Systems
Feedback, Modeling,
Tracking

Persistent
Reinforcing

Cheerleader
Monitor
Coach

ENTRY

Clarifying Situation
Deciding to Mediate

Validating
Empathizing, Mirroring
Choices
Trustbuilding

Sensitive
Stimulating
Trustworthy

Counselor
Catalyst

Consultant
Researcher
Planner

Logical
Intuitive
Patient

Understanding Frameworks
Analyzing
Interpreting

Interviewing
Observing
Using Secondary Sources

DIAGNOSIS

Synthesizer
Option Generator
Scapegoat

Precise
Methodical
Open-minded

Teacher
Confronter
Process-regulator

Nurturing, Flexible,
Good-humored
Objective, Articulate

Listening
Interpreting
Persuading

AGREEMENTS

Using Creative Strategies
Assessing Options
Making Precise Agreements

Seeing Alternatives
Fine Tuning Agreements
Specifying Format

Identifying Interests and Common Ground,
Fractionating Issues
Balancing Power, Re-framing, Breaking Deadlocks, Generating Options

NEGOTIATION

MEDIATION STAGE II: DIAGNOSIS/UNPACKING THE CONFLICT

Sarah to her manager: "I just can't get Sam's cooperation on our new project. We are supposed to be co-workers on this and he resists everything new I try to do."

Manager: "He always resists things. Just tell him to get on board."

THE MANAGER IS MAKING THE FATAL BUT ALL-TOO-COMMON MISTAKE OF acting before diagnosing a conflict. In the rush to fix things, most people hear one side of a conflict and then take action, rather than gathering all the information necessary to properly diagnose the complete conflict dynamics. As a result, the dispute re-emerges and embroils people repeatedly. The first indication of a conflict is like the proverbial tip of the iceberg — there is far more lurking below the surface.

Uncovering the not-so-obvious elements of the conflict is the second stage of the mediation process: diagnosis. While many people overlook creating safety for participants during the entry stage, even more people tend to sidestep understanding the underlying conflict issues, impatiently declaring, "We don't have time for all that; we have too much to do," or, "People just need to grow up and act rational. This is the real world. Feelings don't belong at work."

When an organization shoves conflicts aside in the interest of expediency, it is creating a time bomb without a clock. No one can safely handle the time bomb nor predict when it will explode. Organizations spend enormous amounts of time, energy and money cleaning up the messes created after long-ignored or hidden issues erupt.

We advocate spending time to accurately diagnose the dispute. Then the real problems may be solved. The entire organization may reach its goals. Working relationships and the working environment are enhanced for everyone.

We believe taking the time to unpack the complexities of a conflict is time well spent and, in the long run, far more efficient and productive than shoving conflicts aside or ignoring them in the hope that they will go away. Here are some guidelines to help you with this important, challenging work.

If it is clear who ought to be at the table and if the complexity and intensity of the conflict are manageable, you may decide to begin the mediation after the entry work. You have participants set ground rules, list issues and decide on the agenda. Your diagnosis is structured into the mediation. If the conflict boils up again after you have begun, more diagnosis work can be done in individual caucuses.

However, most conflicts need a more formal diagnosis in order to structure the mediation more efficiently. This also gives the conflicting parties a chance to vent their anger, hurt and frustration. By draining off some hostility, occasionally they are able to re-frame their positions as well.

Completing an effective, formal diagnosis requires understanding these key concepts:

- ▸ The difference between personalities and communication patterns.
- ▸ The central elements of conflict.
- ▸ The different methods of collecting information.
- ▸ The elements of mediation planning.

Patterns, Not Personalities

Those with no training in conflict management seek to explain organizational disputes through personality analysis, usually focusing on only one of the parties: Ed is a "resistant" personality, which is why he gets into struggles with Sarah. And for many people, affixing labels constitutes a full and complete analysis. From this point of view, a conflict exists only because of one person's aberrant personality. Accurate conflict diagnosis, by contrast, examines the communication patterns, not the personalities, of the individuals involved. When two people are involved in a conflict, they each contribute to the problem. Sarah may systematically exclude Ed from meetings where decisions are made that affect him — so he resists Sarah's decisions and her authority. When included in the meetings, however, Ed may be argumentative and non-collaborative — so Sarah excludes him. In all conflicts, the parties are intertwined; each makes choices that contribute to the ongoing struggle.

It is interesting that people who have not had professional training in personality diagnosis rush to use personality labels. Professionals, such as clinical psychologists, insist on extensive assessment before labeling people, yet managers and co-workers are quick to call others difficult, hostile or crazy.

When a person labels another's personality, it doesn't illuminate the conflict patterns. The label serves only to lay the blame on one party. Let's face it — if all the people called "imbalanced" and "crazy" were institutionalized, there would hardly be anyone left to run an organization. One key to conflict *misdiagnosis* is concluding that only one party is responsible because that person has some underlying personality flaw. Personality labels stop us from seeking the choices and actions both parties take to keep the conflict going — the conflict dynamics.

Conflict Elements

Diagnosing a conflict requires knowing what questions to ask and what to observe. Both process elements and organizational elements must be understood for a clear picture of the dispute. Otherwise, you are likely to collect information on some relevant issues but miss others that may be the key that unlocks the dispute. Here is an overview of the elements of conflict that form the basis for interviewing, observing and analyzing conflicts.

Process Elements

We define conflict as "an expressed struggle between interdependent parties who perceive incompatible goals and scarce resources and who interfere with each others' goal attainment."[1] Conflict is an interpersonal event that unfolds because of actions by both parties. Communication dynamics based on perception both create and reflect the conflict elements. First, note that the bedrock for understanding conflict is to take perceptions as reality. The negative images of each other may be "only perceptions," but they fuel the fiery bonds between people.

How is the conflict being expressed?

A conflict is expressed either overtly or covertly.

Overt expressions include such things as:

► Shouting at each other.

► Walking out of meetings.

► Saying ultimatums, threats or "over my dead body" statements.

► Talking to others about the conflict.

Covert expressions include:

► Avoiding the other.

► Refusing to talk to the other.

► Joking and changing the subject.

► Passive resistance and passive-aggressive behavior like reluctantly complying, refusing to cooperate or other forms of non-responsiveness: missing meetings, being late on reports, forgetting appointments.

► Physical ailments: heart attacks, muscle spasms, ulcers, colitis and other internalization of external stress.

The way the struggle is expressed can push the conflict into one of four directions: escalation, de-escalation, maintaining the status quo or avoidance.[2] See the Struggle Spectrum, page 18.

As a mediator, you need to ask:

▸ In what direction is the conflict moving, and with what results?

▸ What behaviors are pushing the conflict in that direction?

▸ How can I behave to move a destructive conflict in a different direction?

Remember that no direction is inherently good or bad. The issue is matching the direction to the desired outcome of the conflict. Consider the non-profit agency where conflict is often avoided except for periodic eruptions that result in a loss of trust and esteem. Anyone who speaks of the underlying issues is identified as the one with a performance problem, the one who is not a team player and generally becomes the scapegoat. In mediation, all participants will have to examine their behavior in order to create a positive outcome. To begin to break the deadlock, the mediator may move to escalate the conflict, perhaps by providing feedback on the avoidance and scapegoating patterns. Identifying underlying patterns tends to escalate the conflict temporarily, then helps reduce the intensity.

On the other extreme, in some high-tech industries, conflicts are consistently escalated. Team members take rigid positions, argue about whose solution is right and who gets credit and may belittle one division of the organization to inflate another. Here, the mediator needs to de-escalate the conflict and may even suggest avoiding some specific issues.

How are the parties interdependent?

In all these situations, the disputants are interdependent in some way — or else they wouldn't have a conflict. Of course, the degree of interdependence varies in conflicts. But each party needs something from the other — a product delivered, information, cooperation, or respect.

One gauge to the intensity of a dispute is how the parties try to convince themselves they aren't interdependent. For example, "I don't need him" translates into "I am so frustrated and upset at his lack of cooperation that I'm going to pretend I don't need him." Attempts to convince themselves that they are free agents reflect how interdependent and stuck people feel. The most intense conflicts happen when people need a great deal from each other and are highly interdependent.

In assessing the interdependence, it is crucial to focus on what disputants have in common. Both in the diagnosis and negotiation phases, this focus softens the ground on which the parties stand, often making it possible to move forward in seemingly unsolvable conflicts. Common ground need not be just the issues central to the conflict but can include personal history, families, values that all hold dear, common misery and people that the disputants want to please or at least not offend. The power of common ground to bind people together, to help them understand they live in the same world and can affect each other for good or ill is not to be underestimated.[3]

What are the parties seeking?

Conflict participants always perceive some scarcity of resources — money, promotions, time, interpersonal inclusion, credibility or some other desirable commodity. And, they see their goals as incompatible: if he gets what he wants, that means I can't get what I want.

There are three types of goals — (1) content goals, (2) relational goals and (3) procedural goals. The *content goals* of a conflict include such things as salary, getting the job done, promotions and other factors that are observable and concrete. Content issues are actually disputes over limited resources — there is only so much time, so many management positions, so much money. *Usually content goals are the only ones openly discussed in organizations.*

Relational goals, by contrast, are subjective things such as being included by others, being treated with respect, being appreciated and recognized, having enough influence to feel competent and get the job done. When someone says, "I just don't want to work with him anymore. I can't stand how he treats me," you are hearing a relational interest.

Eventually, all conflicts include elements of power and self-esteem.[4] When Wes tells you, "I think we need to find someone else to head up the project team," and then you both get into a dispute, issues of power and self-esteem are readily apparent.

Relational goals are not limited resources, but people often fight about them as if they were, acting as if only a few people are allowed to have esteem or power or appreciation. There may be conflict over ways of having these relational goals met, but *all* can have esteem; everyone can be liked. It makes little sense to say, "If I give you my love, then I have less for myself." The giving of love generates more. The same is true of power — the more people are empowered, the more is available for the entire group. All indicators suggest that shared power (empowerment) generates more energy, productivity and quality in organizations. Workforces that feel empowered provide more creative solutions to daily work issues, share information readily and pull together in crises rather than assigning blame.[5] But we have been taught to act as if sharing power in organizations undermines authority.

Procedural goals are concerned with how things get done — a desire for fair play, equal treatment, appropriate talk time and other rules of operation. For example, everyone may want a high performing team but disagree about how often team members should meet to create the cohesion such a team requires.

We have found that one reason conflicts can be so destructive is that people conflict over the wrong thing. They misdiagnose the goals and interests in the dispute. Salary may be discussed heatedly, but the real issue is being recognized and valued by the manager. The employee has only a salary increase as an indicator or symbol of his or her value. Then, even when a salary increase is given, the additional money is only a short-term motivator since the rest of the year includes no recognitions, no "thank-you's" or celebrations of success. Then, of course, both the manager and employee feel betrayed when complaints continue. Many agreements do not endure because the real issues and goals in the organization were never diagnosed and discussed.

A word of caution: When a manager "slides to solutions" without diagnosing the conflict, the solutions will not work. Instant solutions do work *for the manager*, but not for the conflict parties. Consider the project leader who formed a cross-functional team to support project planning but ignored the history of hostility among many of the functional areas. Team meetings sounded more like sparring matches for the winning idea than a cooperative effort for mutual goals. The leader simply insisted on cooperation and trained the team in good listening skills — a solution that did nothing to air and resolve the real, underlying issues.

If the solution isn't tailored for the parties in the conflict, the dispute grows more toxic and destructive each time it recycles. The solution has to work for those in conflict or else it isn't a solution. They are the ones who start and maintain the conflict.

To know if the issues have been diagnosed accurately, use the "Three Times" Rule

A general rule of thumb is that, in organizations, relational goals are translated into content or procedural issues. Since relational issues are not discussed directly, the content or procedural conflicts keep recycling, surfacing most often at budget time or at critical points in the project. In the example above, salary becomes an annual issue, giving little temporary satisfaction to the employee and creating a great deal of irritation to the manager. More than likely, there are other, more effective ways of meeting the employee's need to be valued, if it were accurately diagnosed. Dealing with the wrong issue renders agreements unworkable.

The Three Times Rule: If you have a conflict over the same content issue more than three times, that means you have misdiagnosed the real issues.[6]

How are the parties interfering with each other?

In all conflicts, the parties interfere with one another's goal attainment. You oppose Judy's appointment to the special task force and she spreads rumors that you are taking extra time away from work. The destructiveness of conflict is directly proportional to how much time and energy disputants invest in getting back at, belittling or reducing the power of the other party. In repetitive, destructive conflicts, the goal shifts from wanting to do a good job to making sure the other parties don't accomplish their goals.

Once the elements of a conflict are clear and the patterns can be diagnosed, you can intervene to alter the conflict elements. Basically, the mediator's job is to *transform the conflict elements* so that mutual interference is turned into joint problem solving.

- ▸ You can work with the conflict participants to change the way they express themselves, so that mutual listening takes place.

- ▸ You can help them clarify their real goals so that agreements endure.

- ▸ You can help them re-focus on what they want and, perhaps, how they can assist each other in meeting their common goals instead of spending their energy interfering with each other.

- ▸ You can remind them of their actual interdependence — how they need and can help each other.

  OR

- ▸ You can clarify their lack of interdependence and help them see how they can get their needs met elsewhere.

OR

► You can help them regulate how much they depend on each other. There may be situations in which one party depends too much on the other; hence problems of power continually erupt.

At the end of this chapter, you will find a Conflict Process Diagnostic Guide that summarizes these elements and provides questions you can use to assess the process elements of a conflict.

Organizational Elements

Discussing the difference between personalities and communication patterns, we noted that behavior is most often a function of a system, not just the personalities of individuals. In a similar vein, we have found that structure, work flow, reward systems and other organizational variables can either support or hinder people's ability to make effective, durable agreements.

An appreciation of the organizational context of a conflict helps you understand the constraints and pressures on people in the work setting as you unravel disputes. Conflict occurs in an organizational arena that brings its own forces to bear on the resolution of the conflict. In turn, the organization exists in a larger economic and cultural environment that often has an impact on the way conflict is handled.

Production workers in a mid-size company were bickering among themselves, starting to use more overtime while also reducing productivity for the hours they were working. The request was to mediate the conflict among the workers to increase production. Upon closer examination, we found that the top management, not being clear about its strategic direction, had promised customers delivery dates based on an unrealistic evaluation of production capacity. Product delivery was also delayed because there was no project plan with check points. The marketing people, feeling ignored by the production people, found fault with some aspects of the product at the last minute, causing costly, time-consuming delays. Furthermore, a norm of this post-entrepreneurial company was to avoid any direct confrontation. Instead of stopping to take the time to solve problems, they simply worked harder and longer if necessary. In fact, the heroes of the organizational culture were those who, under enormous pressure, stepped in to rescue a project at the last minute. As the company grew, conflict avoidance and heroic stances no longer sufficed.

The combined pressures on the production workers were enormous, and often out of their control. To consider only their behavior in mediation — without examining these organizational pressures — could provide only temporary relief at best. The biggest production issue would go unsolved. The production team *could* work on their conflict norms, *could* insist on a more formal project plan with marketing and *could* decide to set their boundaries around work and refuse to be exhausted heroes — but this would mean putting their jobs and compensation at risk. Resolving the conflict at the production level could also pressure top management to solve the management issues. But the overall strategic direction, in terms of the contracts the company accepted, was out of the hands of the production people. Hence, a thorough resolution of the production issue involved considering more aspects of the company system than just the conflictual behavior of the production workers.

This example points out the need for several cautions about mediating organizational conflict. First, organizational disputes often masquerade as interpersonal conflicts. As the previous story showed, focusing only on individual conflicts prevents looking at the larger system and stymies efforts at creating enduring agreements.

Second, organizational disputes often erupt because of power differences. When people at the high-power end can't (or won't) deal with their differences, the differences are magnified as they grow at the lower end of power. Or, to use the more colloquial expression, "shit rolls downhill," and those in the lower rungs get tagged as complainers or troublemakers. This dynamic, called horizontal violence, often appears among lower-power groups in organizations and cultures.

Secretarial pools often absorb tension from many levels above, cannot confront the source of the pressure because of their position in the organization and release their tension in conflicts with each other. A good rule of thumb is that when the vertical conflict has not been addressed, then horizontal conflict — with low-power people fighting each other — erupts. Then, of course, the low-power group is asked to "please fix your problem" — another form of blaming the victim.[7]

Power differences also can be a result of status in a particular setting. Nurses are asked to improve their communication instead of asking the hospital to confront the way they are treated by doctors. In companies driven by research and development, marketing personnel are often asked to improve their skills instead of dealing with the real conflict, which stems from their relative status compared to the high-status researchers. Mid-level managers often feel squeezed between complying with the top and trying to meet the needs of the bottom, especially in times of major change.

Finally, culturally disempowered groups — women, people of color or of a certain religious group, those with a different sexual preference or those with physical disabilities — are often the scapegoats, identified as the ones in need of change. The scapegoats have neither the power nor often the ability to confront the higher-power groups, the ones defining them as the problem. In organizations, scapegoats are often identified, harassed and eventually fired. But conflicts continue and the system finds another scapegoat. This dynamic enables the system to continue avoiding looking at the systemic effects of exclusion and frustration.

The emerging goals of managing diversity and empowering the work force necessitate a close examination of these systemic effects. Merely focusing on the interpersonal conflicts fails to provide a clear and accurate understanding of the organizational issues surrounding a conflict and blocks the possibility of finding interventions and solutions that work.

One more caution about organizational disputes: repetitive disputes often mirror the unspoken underside of the organizational culture. People will even acknowledge that they don't know why they are acting in a particular way. "It's not like me," they say — and then continue. Questions that unearth the unspoken messages may illuminate these seemingly mysterious eruptions. The unspoken may include certain kinds of feelings that are constantly suppressed by the organization's norms or, perhaps, reflect the values of the organization's founder.

For instance, sexuality is a taboo subject in many churches. So the most disruptive disputes will likely emerge over sexuality, sexual behavior and sexual preference. In many corporations, feelings of all kinds are taboo. Hence, polarized, under-the-table disputes are often driven by unexpressed emotions — who is included and who is excluded, who has power, who feels valued and so on. In most non-profit groups, the unspeakable shadow side is power — people wanting influence while thinking they should not. Seemingly unexplainable conflict erupts when the shadow cannot be expressed and yet has enormous emotional power. People usually pick fights over content issues (hiring the minister, salary increases that symbolize being cared for, arguments about "the good of the client") that symbolize the power issues when people cannot openly discuss the unspeakables in the organizational culture.

One role of the mediator is to help speak the unspeakable. But because the shadow is dangerous territory, the mediator has to frame issues carefully and only approach the unspeakables after some trust has been built.

We have found it often helps to use images and metaphors when addressing the unspeakable issues. When the leaders of an organization see themselves as rugged, individualistic cowboys out to tame the Wild West, for instance, the shadow issues probably involve feelings, collaboration and any "soft" issues in the workforce. A mediator might use some humor by playing with the prevailing metaphor, asking how cowboys might communicate to round up the strays or other ways cowboys might find for taming the maverick horses other than breaking them. Re-framing, a technique detailed in the next chapter, can also be helpful in dealing with shadow issues. See pages 134–138.

Here are the seven key elements for diagnosing organizational conflict. We will examine each and explore their implications for negotiating and reaching agreements.

The Organizational Elements Diagnostic Guide at the end of this chapter summarizes these elements and provides questions you can use to assess the organizational context of conflict.

1. Organizational culture

Culture has to do with the understood and often unspoken values and norms in an organization. It is expressed in terms of artifacts like the building structure, art and kinds of company activities as well as the expectations for appropriate behavior and style of interacting.

Of special concern as you diagnose the conflict and plan the intervention are the cultural norms for managing conflict. The basic question is, what types of conflict behavior are supported and sanctioned by the organizational culture? For example, people in a company may need to be open and direct to clarify and manage simmering conflicts, but hesitate to do so because the culture values the appearance of harmony. Or two people in a law firm may need to cooperate to increase their mutual business, but hesitate to do so since status in the firm is earned by appearing competitive, tough and uncompromising. In one law firm, two principal parties reached an agreement, then discussed how to "appear uncooperative" in front of the other partners while retaining their newfound cooperation with each other for resolving differences. They agreed first to meet privately and resolve differences that emerged and then to make agreements with one another on how to act during the overall partnership meetings. This workable solution allowed them to cooperate within a culture that sanctioned only competition, but did not address the norms of the whole firm, since the system was not the focus at that time.

Every organization has unspoken norms for how conflict should be handled. One private non-profit organization we worked with had a history of decisive one-man rule from the executive director, yet the management team was embroiled in continual dispute because the top-down decisions were wreaking havoc in each of their departments. After the management team negotiated some of the specific disputes, the members then agreed to delineate areas where "one-man rule" would still operate and to let the executive director take credit for some team decisions that were arrived at collaboratively. We also helped them slowly change from a one-man autocracy to a culture of cooperation, joint decision making and consensus. The past culture cannot be completely disregarded when implementing newfound agreements. Consider the prevailing organizational culture and adapt to it, even as you work to transform it.

Often the founder of the organization has a profound and prevailing influence on how conflict is handled. In one family-run business, the founder wanted things to be smooth and also wanted to work through difficulties that arose with the family members. His desire to keep the family members close while working out the conflicts made it possible to convene the entire family and negotiate solutions to the problems. Had he felt that conflict was bad, a family member might have been fired.

Felix, the president and founder of another organization, continued to have enormous influence even after his death. While he was alive, people gained influence in the company by forming one-on-one coalitions with him. After his death, instead of working out existing conflicts, board members would preface their remarks by claiming they knew what Felix would have wanted since they had known him so well. The Board was constantly deadlocked since they only argued about Felix's preference — which they obviously could not check out — instead of their own present-tense interests. Felix's ghost had to be laid to rest before the conflict could be managed.

It's also possible to use dysfunctional organizational norms to create workable solutions — as we did working with the faculty of a law enforcement academy. Their communication style, characterized by a constant barrage of put-down humor, blocked effective agreements. Attempts to change this norm, deeply embedded in the "cop culture," were futile. Instead, they agreed to appoint a "Zap Control Officer" who would blow an earsplitting whistle when the humor began to block decision making in each meeting. This humorous solution used their own norms to constrain their blocking behavior.

It is often possible for a team of people or an entire organization to make their conflict norms explicit, to examine their effectiveness and to make agreements to align the norms with the group's purposes so there are no unnecessary barriers to their agreements. Alignment as a group or an organization has the most power to create durable agreements.

This can be as simple as asking the group members to identify how they usually manage conflict, to select the norms that are functional, to create new ones to replace the dysfunctional ones and to use mechanisms like staff meetings to monitor the new norms until they become second nature. This change takes thoughtfulness and energy — but usually no more than the destructive conflict has taken.

Occasionally, the group may need to acquire new skills — as a group. In *The Fifth Discipline*, Peter Senge distinguishes between individual and collective learning.[8] Collective learning involves making agreements as a team and understanding the feelings and behaviors that support the team efforts — which are not simply a combination of individual efforts. Although individuals need certain skills, sending them away to learn team skills is like having a musician practice alone to learn to be part of a great jazz ensemble, Senge observes.

2. Structure of work

Often the way work is structured precipitates unnecessary conflict. In many companies, the successful rollout of a product depends on the early cooperation of cross-functional teams, yet work is structured so that teams in various departments are isolated and operate independently. In this situation, teams will keep encountering the same conflicts until the structure is changed. Cross-functional and self-managing work teams offer changes that will bring the organizational structure into alignment with its goals. Of course, team members must learn new norms and find new ways of managing their daily conflicts in direct and timely ways, but the conflicts will be real ones — actual problems that can be solved — rather than recurring conflicts that are artifacts of the structure.

3. Third-party representation

The bargaining table may have people who represent other groups — their team, a union, the city council, top management and so on. Be aware that group cohesion is often built by having common enemies. Consequently, groups can push their representatives to win for them, which increases the competitive behavior of the disputants. The representatives face a special dilemma — needing to consider collaborative solutions with others at the table, while also exacting "the pound of flesh" demanded to satisfy their constituents and maintain status with them.

Once the pressures that each bargainer feels are understood, then measures can be taken to moderate or accommodate them. Some possibilities might be:

- The mediation could be in a place that is more private and reduces public pressure to perform.

- Before coming to the table, the representatives could reach agreements with their groups about the relative importance of winning versus accomplishing the group's goals. In essence, the first mediation sessions would be between the representatives and their teams.

- Representatives at the table might agree that a certain kind of display is necessary to satisfy constituent groups. That symbolic display could be built into the mediation process so the representatives do not lose face with their groups. Mediation participants may agree to certain concessions merely because some of the representatives need to satisfy their group and/or save face. This is often a consideration with union or public policy negotiations.

▸ Disputants can strategize with each other about ways to persuade constituent groups to accept an agreement that is mutually beneficial. The disputants understand the need to cooperate but must convince their groups they are not collaborating with the enemy.

▸ Finally, it may be necessary — and even preferable — to bring all the groups together so that all are involved in the mediation. Large group designs bring all the key stakeholders into the room to establish common ground, to explore the issues and to reach agreement.[9]

4. Leadership — positive and negative

People in organizations tend to emulate the style of the leaders, which means that leaders serve as powerful role models for constructive or destructive conflict. If the mediator can remind disputants of the preferred constructive styles of credible leaders, those in conflict may have an incentive for moving to workable solutions. Formal or informal leaders who are skilled in mediation may also be involved in the actual mediation. Less formally, disputants may push for workable solutions when they want to maintain credibility with their peers. The same is true when they want to avoid negative public opinion or to create agreements that would be supported by public opinion. Even reminding disputants of organizational heroes and heroines who have created workable solutions in the face of sometimes impossible odds can provide hope and incentive for moving forward.

The negative aspect of this phenomenon is that people also use visible leaders as excuses for why they can't be constructive. "How can we possibly be productive when the leaders aren't perfect?" is their cry. In this case, remind those in conflict of what they, themselves, have the power to change, separate from what has to be discussed with their leaders. Fractionating the conflict this way allows people to move forward and may suggest follow-up work to be done within the larger organizational context.

5. Reward structures

For the greatest productivity within an organization, rewards ought to match desired behavior. Rewarding individuals through a hierarchical ranking system will not increase cooperative, team behavior, for instance. Unnecessary conflicts are created when people suppress an impulse toward heroic behavior in order to work for the team, only to find later that highly competitive individual contributors are given all the awards and recognition, even though everyone is constantly deluged with company rhetoric to be a good team member. In the same vein, in the current milieu of total quality, high performing teams and diverse workforces require that managers move from being experts to facilitators and coordinators. Many companies recognize the need to shift and yet still promote and reward those managers who control, manage top-down and foster individual versus collective action. This lack of consistency or alignment creates a climate that fosters conflict and dishonesty and may even promote physical illness.

Organizations fail to realize that people stay conflicted internally trying to meet incompatible demands. Internal conflict results in irritation that usually emerges in conflict with managers and/or in general irritability toward co-workers.

Also, people may do what they are rewarded for while pretending to comply with the public rhetoric. A common example is to continue competing with colleagues while talking teamwork. Then conflicts emerge between people and teams who are operating on different assumptions about what is required of them. In the final analysis, organizations lose the energy of people who are busy trying to figure out what is required of them and how to get it done so they can be rewarded.

The mediator must at least be aware of the prevailing reward system, so that agreements can acknowledge it and take that reality into account. Disputants may decide to do what needs to be done in spite of the reward system, but they must do so knowingly in order to avoid feeling betrayed later on. Or it may be that, given the reward structure, certain agreements simply will not stick. If disputants can acknowledge the problematic nature of the reward system, they can decide to relinquish some goals in order to be rewarded for others. Finally, it may emerge that the reward structure is one of the key conflict issues to be negotiated.

6. Conflict management procedures

Each organization has a built-in system of dispute resolution, whether it's positive or negative. On one end of the spectrum are organizations that ignore conflict, hope it will never erupt and try to stamp it out like a range fire when it flares up. When a fire erupts, people run in panic to the manager, who assumes the role of forest ranger. Instead of bringing the disputants together, the ranger/manager tries to stifle the flames quickly, talking to each party individually, then arbitrating some sort of a decision. This procedure often fails to deal with the emotional aspect of the dispute or the possibility of joint solutions — and certainly does nothing to build the parties' confidence in their ability to deal with conflict in the future. In addition, this form of arbitration almost invariably creates winner(s) and loser(s) — which adds to the overall tension in the system.

At the other end of the spectrum are organizations that set up a system for dispute resolution — usually larger corporations, government agencies and the like. With a system for dispute resolution, the *process* of resolving disputes is specified. For example, the employee handbook may stipulate the following process to address difficulty with a supervisor:

1. Discuss and try to resolve the grievance with the immediate supervisor.

2. File a written reaction to the meeting and meet with the next level supervisor.

3. If the informal meeting does not work, file a formal written appeal with a grievance committee.

4. If necessary, hold a formal hearing with the grievance committee.

5. If the employee is still not satisfied, appeal to an internal appeals committee.

6. At the end of the in-house process, if the conflict is still not resolved, pursue a court action.

Having this type of dispute resolution mechanism in place will naturally have an impact on the way conflicts are acted out. Employees often experience such procedures as highly visible and legalistic, with sides collecting evidence to support their point of view. If the disputants perceive the procedures as too costly in terms of time, money, reputation or image, or see them as likely to produce an outcome that favors one side over another, they will be reluctant to use them. On the other hand, if the processes are heavily used while similar conflicts keep emerging, this is a sign that the central issue still remains and the procedures may need to be reviewed.[10]

The mediator, whether internal or external to the organization, must be aware of the normal procedures and try to interrupt the spiral of conflict at the earliest possible point. Developing new norms and procedures for handling conflicts may also need to be a part of the mediation process. In striving to handle everyday conflict more directly, some organizations have instituted an internal mediation service, training people in all levels of the organization and making them available to handle disputes. A similar process in schools trains a group of kids who then wear "mediator hats" on the playground. When students are the primary resource for settling conflicts, the teachers rarely have to intervene and the students develop the necessary skills and confidence to handle their own conflicts.

No single set of procedures will work uniformly to constructively manage conflict, but each organization should examine its procedures and ask:

- ► Do these procedures facilitate constructive conflict management?

- ► Do we have a coordinated system for managing disputes?

- ► Are we able to handle the dispute resolution in-house or do we find that we have to continually use outsiders to manage disputes that arise as a normal part of the work environment?

- ► Do we have employees and supervisors adequately trained in conflict management skills so we can improve, over time, our in-house skills in conflict management?

7. Economic and cultural environment

It is important to understand that community attitudes can support constructive or competitive conflict resolution. In the West, for instance, the attitude of tough individualism often prevails and, whatever the agreement, disputants may need to look as if they have emerged the winner. In the South where graciousness is valued, the mediator may want to avoid using the word "conflict" and choose a more euphemistic term, like "problem solving" to describe the situation.

In *The Mediation Process*, Christopher Moore tells of a mining town in which forces in the community support workers striking as well as other ways of showing the bosses that the workers have clout.[11] If strikes are to be avoided in such an environment, the norm of exhibiting power probably has to be maintained, which means the workers may need some way other than strikes to demonstrate their power. The central question is, what forces in this environment will support or defeat this agreement?

If you make an agreement that is counter to the prevailing norms, you need ways to provide buffers for the participants. Otherwise, the cultural norms will slowly take precedence. Often, the cultural milieu may not support conflict management and see it as "soft," in which case it would be wise to present agreements in a way that focuses on the struggle. A press release might say, "The negotiators, after many hours of struggling and times of serious disagreements, finally managed to forge a solution that works for everyone."

Or the disputants may want to be seen as rational and professional, as was the case in a public sector conflict we mediated. Reminding several disputants how they would appear to the community if they refused to cooperate was what produced movement.

Whatever the specifics, it's important to enlist forces that will enhance supportive forces and moderate restraining forces when your goal is to reach agreements that will work over time.

There are several general implications of considering these organizational elements. First, often before you begin mediation, you need to know from the participants' bosses, and others with power in the organization, what their stake is in the dispute and any parameters they have for the agreement. You may need an agreement to mediate not only between the two disputants, for example, but also with their managers who have a high investment in the outcome. Then you will know from the outset the expectations, parameters, support and obstacles the disputants can expect from their managers.

Second, acknowledging the organizational constraints may be all you, the mediator, can do and you must simply help the disputants work with and around the organizational pressures as best you can. The distinction between a dilemma and problem is important here. A problem can be solved; a dilemma can only be managed. Be clear about which you are working with.

Third, if the effects of the conflict are so embedded in the organizational system that yet another attempt at solution will likely be futile, consider getting representatives from all parts of the system in the room. This way, you can work with the immediate issues of concern as well as long-term systemic changes to prevent recurring conflict patterns in the future.

Finally, whenever possible, help pairs or teams or whole systems examine and align their conflict management practices with their goals. The more a system is in alignment, the less energy will be spent on unproductive, unnecessary disputes and more on finding creative solutions to here-and-now, solvable issues.

Collecting Information

With an understanding of the process and organizational conflict elements, the next step is collecting information about the dispute. Here we are describing the formal and full-blown process of diagnosis. But keep in mind the idea that these steps can sometimes be accomplished informally and quickly, depending on the dispute. Being fully aware of the details minimizes the chance of inadvertently missing some steps and failing to understand why the mediation fails.

Collecting data includes interviewing, observing and using secondary sources.

Interviewing

You interview to find the patterns in the conflict — not to decide who is at fault. In most conflicts, the protagonists attempt to convince everyone that the conflict is the fault of the other. Therefore, more faultfinding from someone trying to act as a mediator isn't helpful — clear, systemwide diagnosis is. And, of course, interviewing has other purposes as well. In an interview you:

- Gather vital information from the conflict participants and others.
- Build rapport with the parties and signal your interest in assisting them.
- Coach people on how to present their ideas and get their interests met.

▸ Begin the process of helping people change so they can manage their dispute.

In terms of our Mediation Wheel, interviewing is best conducted from a "soft" perspective—being flexible, open, receptive, showing empathy and concern for people struggling with one another. If you find yourself deciding partway through interviewing that one side is to blame, you have lost the receptive, open perspective needed for quality data gathering. Remember that each person in a conflict contributes something.

One of us recently intervened in an ongoing, three-year dispute within an organization where one employee was said to have a performance problem. A distillation of the interview notes on the following page illustrates the contribution of each person to the dispute. John and Carl are in an organization that gives them considerable autonomy and power.

These notes illustrate how interviewing can uncover layers in a conflict. In each conflict, the "presenting problem," in this case Pat's performance, is only part of the dynamics. If you are looking for "fault," you could focus on any one of the players with almost equal justification. This conflict was managed by (1) getting John and Carl to decide jointly what kind of system they wanted; (2) enhancing Mary's responsibility as office manager by having her lead a meeting with John, Carl and the other staff; (3) addressing the performance problems Pat evidenced; and (4) re-aligning the work assignments so Pat no longer reported to John.

Conflicts demand multiple solutions. Because everyone contributes to the patterns, the situation can't be corrected by only one person changing. As a result, it is crucial in the interviewing stage to stay open, be receptive, look for patterns and joint contributions to the difficulties and refuse to point the finger of blame at any one person.

Notes on ABC Organization

John (Vice President): inflexible, wants to control others, not responsive to the five staff members, wants an integrated system but is apparently incapable of working with others to bring it about. No one likes him; all find him difficult to work with.

Carl (Vice President): open, humorous, staff likes him. He has decided that under no circumstances can he work with John, the other V.P. Staff likes Carl but he is no longer willing to work with John and refuses to meet "even one more time" with John because he is so frustrated with John's lack of responsiveness and communication skills. He works very hard, likes the staff, but won't address the conflict between him and John in a direct manner. He wants a totally separate system for the two of them.

Mary (Office Manager): will not confront John or Carl about their disagreement on (1) integrated or (2) separate systems of operation. She works hard with staff to juggle the conflicting demands from John and Carl. She wants to please others but they see her as less effective than she sees herself. Staff resents her for not doing enough of the clerical work.

Pat (Staff member): has a performance problem; John dislikes her and has always wanted her replaced. Early on, he brought a complaint to her attention, yet it turned out the complaint was about another woman named Pat who no longer is in the office. She does the system a favor by bringing this conflict to a head. She is the only staff member responsible to both John and Carl and this structural confusion sets her up as a target for their dispute. John wants her fired and Carl defends her, saying John has "singled her out."

Other staff: want to stay out of the conflict but overall see equal contributions on the part of John, Carl, Mary and Pat to the bad stuff going on. Most have not told their supervisors or the two Vice Presidents about their concerns and are reluctant to engage. They see Pat as in an impossible position, but hold her partly responsible and do not want to share her work or take over her job. They just want to do their jobs and go home.

Basically, the principles of interviewing are these:

Stay open

Be receptive, look for patterns rather than fault.

Look for perceptual data

Disputes are driven by peoples' differing views of issues and events. When one person says Jim has a performance problem, Jim will be able to detail the shabby treatment he has received. Your job isn't to decide which perspective is correct; rather, it is to see how the perceptions interlock to produce destructive patterns. Remember, the data are (1) behaviors by each person and (2) differing perceptions and explanations of those behaviors.

Use the "Criticism-Opposite" Rule

We criticize whatever is the opposite of what we want. For example, if Roy accuses Bill of being distant, intellectual and removed from reality, Roy probably wants connection, positive feedback and human warmth. Find each person's values, based on their criticism of the other.

Look for underlying interests

Positions are attempted solutions to problems. Demands for a salary increase, a personal computer or a new office may symbolize the recognition they feel they deserve. Every fixed position — "I have to have X" — reflects a desire to solve a problem in a fixed, non-negotiable way. Behind each of these positions is an interest. Often, because of our cultural norms, people can't ask for what they really want.

Business partners Mike and Sam began a mediation with Sam demanding $30,000 for his share of the new operation. During mediation we discovered that Sam felt left out of some new plans and saw himself as a mover and shaker in tandem with Mike. During the interview stage, Sam was asked, "I understand you want the $30,000. What would that do for you?" This uncovered the interest propelling Sam to the rigid demand for $30,000 — he simply wanted involvement and recognition.

After mediation, as part of their agreement, Sam offered to do free training for Mike's group in Hawaii if Mike would pay his expenses. The training helped Mike's new group and Sam got recognition for his training talents — quite a change from demanding $30,000!

Use the interview to chip away at negative perceptions

When someone says, "He only wants to control me," you can re-frame it as "He must be afraid of change if he has to act in such a domineering manner." In general, you can translate "personality" attributions into interests.

Who to interview

Interview everyone with a significant stake in the conflict; those with critical information; those with power or perceived power; and all important decision makers and those who need to carry out any decisions reached. After you have interviewed all parties the conflict dynamics should be clear.

The sequencing or timing of interviews is also important

While there are no right answers, there are several issues to consider.

Who is most powerful in the dispute?

If these people would be highly offended if not interviewed first to signal their importance and position, be aware of this and make a decision accordingly. Also, these people may need to be interviewed first in order to assure those lower in power that you won't "tell on them."

Who is least powerful?

By first interviewing the parties who are the least powerful or in most danger by not cooperating, you signal your concern to them. They are more likely to be cooperative if they think you have not loaded the deck against them by talking to the higher-power people first.

Whose cooperation could be used to influence others?

Sometimes, interviewing those with high credibility or informal influence serves to encourage others who are reluctant to be cooperative.

Who is most likely to talk about the problem?

Sometimes people are so closemouthed about issues that the best choice for first interviews are those who will tell you the truth.

To sidestep some of the inherent traps of deciding who to interview first, consider conducting group interviews. This requires first assessing the degree of hostility among the people and their consequent need for confidentiality. One advantage of a group interview is it also provides a chance to gather observational data at the same time.

Martha, the person who initiated mediation, described her co-worker Helen as controlling and constantly intrusive, saying, "Something must be done. She is so unprofessional." During a group interview, we asked each person to describe the situation. We noticed that during the process, Martha arrogantly contradicted everyone's perceptions. Most of the others were cowed by Martha. Helen was the only one who insisted on her own perceptions. The mediators had to get Martha to own her behavior before any progress could be made. It is often true, as we found in this situation, that the one doing the accusing is also the one controlling.

Mediating multi-party disputes usually means interviewing representatives from the various stakeholders groups. If the conflict is particularly hostile, the first step may be to get agreements from the constituent groups to authorize the representative to be interviewed and to make agreements in their behalf. Omitting this step makes it easy to sabotage agreements later.

If you are unsure of how to start, a set of structured questions like those given in the Organizational Elements Diagnostic Guide at the end of this chapter may be useful. Otherwise, let the participants lead the way to important areas by asking them open-ended questions such as, "How did you experience that?"

One final note. It is critical to transcend your personal biases in interviewing. If you cannot suspend judgment or find yourself thinking "Yep, it really is *his* fault," then you have lost the larger, system-wide view necessary to help. When your biases enter, they are communicated, usually unconsciously, by showing disapproval non-verbally. Unless you remain balanced between the parties and keep a system view, you will coalesce or side with one of the parties and then become a party to the conflict yourself. Coalition-building always exacerbates the conflict. You can be certain that the parties will be monitoring you for any signs of being more sympathetic to one side than the other.

Observation

If you work within the organization, you may be in a good position to observe a conflict. It may occur near your office or you may see it unfold during a meeting. You can observe a conflict between two people, in a group meeting or intergroup meeting or at a company meeting. If you are an outside mediator, you likely will need to attend meetings to observe conflict dynamics. You then can merge observation with interview data (1) to get a clear picture of the conflict elements, (2) to see the productive elements that can increase chances of a positive outcome and (3) to identify the destructive patterns that need to be altered.

There are several principles to remember when you are observing conflict for accurate diagnosis:

Stay behavioral

Notice observable behavior and distinguish that from your fantasy or your inferences about intentions and motives. For example, hearing people raising their voices, you might infer that they are angry, even though raised voices can also mean excitement and commitment. By drawing inferences from the behaviors you observe, you may be accurate, but it is possible that your biases may also be coloring your perception.

Use metaphor and story

This principle may seem to contradict the first one, but only if you confuse story and inference with behavioral data. The quickest overview of the conflict system often comes through images that pop up, either in your mind or from the participants. These can be used to build a story you intentionally create. For instance, one team in conflict characterized itself as wild animals in cages. If you stay with that metaphor to ask questions and observe interactions, you can generate a great deal of important information.

How do the animals communicate? How do they compete & cooperate?	Expressed Struggle
Who is the zoo keeper? Is the door locked?	Power
What do they eat? Is there enough to eat?	Resources
Do they want to stay there or go somewhere else? Where?	Goals
Who/What keeps them from doing what they want?	Interference

> We are all different kinds of wild animals who have been caged for a long time and who have become flabby, out of hop, and not able to survive in the wild. The gate is not locked though we think it is. No one bothers to check anymore. We growl and claw at each other during feeding time because we think there is not enough food to go around. If we could get out, we don't know where we would go.

This story describes a group that has lost its energy and its vision of the future and now fights over what the group perceives as limited resources. They could exercise more power, but then they wouldn't know what to do. They blame their keeper for their situation, even though the keeper doesn't even lock the door. The keeper probably symbolizes their manager or the system in which they are working.

Interventions in this conflict could include creating a vision, expanding the team's sense of what's possible, encouraging them to take risks slowly, contracting with the manager to provide guidance and assistance as the team members become more interdependent.

When people begin to play with a common image, several things happen. They begin to cooperate in generating data — often a first step in unfreezing the dispute. Secondly, they move to a lighter, more playful attitude and provide information that they usually cannot or will not provide when being more rational. Team members begin to work collectively and creatively to solve disputes. Finally, agreeing on a common image sets the stage for generating a preferred image, one that can serve to pull them out of conflict toward a common, collective future.

Images, whether conscious or unconscious, guide our choices and evaluation of behavior. Stories and metaphors can be used in interviews as well as while observing. The mediator can provide an image or ask participants to do so. Either way, notice what image is met with the most enthusiasm or indication of insight — the collective sigh or "aha." If several images are proposed, go with the one that generates the most energy, positive and/or negative.

Team members determined they wanted to move from a M.A.S.H. Unit to a Preventative Health Care Facility while retaining flexibility and a sense of humor.. Their key issues were shifting:

From	To
Crisis	Planning
Disease	Health and healing
Constant stress	An environment with more controlled choices
Sharp division of tasks	Greater collaboration regardless of position

---

Notice patterns

Notice the impact of behaviors on others so you can carefully feed that back to the conflict parties, not making value judgments about whether behaviors are good or bad, but rather about the effects of their behaviors. You might say, "I notice that each time one of you makes an absolute statement with a voice tone that implies the other is foolish, it takes up to half an hour to get back to the identified issues. Unless we want to lengthen the time it takes to reach decisions, you may want to modify those tones."

Use the "Blip Theory" in your diagnosis

When an important issue arises, *something changes*. A face gets flushed, someone stammers, a chair gets pushed back. Something happens. Like on an electrocardiogram, a "Blip" is a sign of an important event.

Lindsey and Janice were discussing the new strategic plan. When the issue of authority came up, Lindsey leaned over, looked more intense and began treating Janice in a rather controlling manner. Blip! When you see a change in non-verbal behavior or in the manner of talking, you have spotted a Blip.

The Blip shows you that a triggering issue has been touched and gives some grounds to begin to speculate about the nature of the conflict. With Lindsey and Janice, the *content issue* was strategic goals; the *relational issue* was power and authority.

In another instance, staff members saw the office manager as not being authoritative enough to coordinate projects. When one staff member said, "We should discuss job assignments," the office manager replied in a defensive tone of voice, "I have done a good job of turning this office around!" Blip! The content issue may be job assignments but the relational issue probably is appreciation. And until appreciation is forthcoming, there will be resistance to clarifying assignments. Or, as is often the case, job assignments may be irrelevant when there is open dialogue about the relational issues and the general need for appreciation.

Blips also provide keys to movement, signalling when the other is receptive to change. Watch for changes that show when a person's interest is tapped. Once people begin to feel they have been heard and their interests noticed, they may relax their posture, open up a dialogue, change their eye contact or alter how they relate to the other conflict party.

Conversely, Blips can signal what items are related to lack of movement or intransigence. When people repeat something, they likely feel they haven't been heard. Careful attention to Blips will key you to the central driving forces of a conflict and point the way to successful resolution.

Notice your own emotional responses

You may be observing a conflict and feel angry. First, check to see if you have been inadvertently pulled into the conflict and want to "set people straight." Then check to see if you are picking up unspoken issues that, until uncovered, will sabotage agreements. In organizational conflicts, participants try to appear as rational as possible since the organizational culture usually has taboos about recognizing feelings and relational needs. If you find yourself feeling angry, make a note to check on who is angry with whom. What history might there be that you are unaware of? If the timing is appropriate, you may say something like, "I'm wondering if there are issues not being expressed. From the way people are carefully controlling their statements, it seems like there may be some issues not on the table, issues having to do with trust or past irritations." Then wait for responses. If such feelings are denied, wait for another time to speak about unexpressed feelings, if they still are present. You have been alerted to watch for this pattern.

Track what you observe to uncover issues

Many people try to figure out the issues and then miss important clues to the conflict as it unfolds. Track the Blips and follow up with questions to find the conflict sub-structure. Watch for clues and then follow up as if you are on a treasure hunt. You are the receiver, not the initiator at this stage.

In one conflict, the mediators could not figure out why a woman manager was so rigid. The other conflict parties, of course, said that the problem was her personality, that she had always been inflexible and would never change. However, noticing she appeared rigid when the topic of her schedule came up was the clue: her concerns were about protecting her time at home with her family. If she agreed to be flexible — which meant working eighteen hours a day the way her teammates were willing to do — she lost protected family time, her most important interest. Indications of interests, not personality analysis, are the focus of mediation.

Diagnose, do not fix

The biggest error in the diagnostic phase is to try to figure out a solution to the problem before completing the full diagnosis. Some mediators become frustrated when they can't find a solution or when one they have suggested is not taken by the disputants. Remember, when issues are clearly understood, the conflict parties will generally construct and keep agreements that work for them. The mediator's job is to help uncover and diagnose the issues.

Secondary sources

Most organizational conflicts come with paper trails. To get a full picture of a dispute, consider secondary sources such as key memos, reports, previous research, financial records, minutes of meetings and press releases. Decide on the sources to look at, based on their importance to the participants. One conflict participant may bring notes he has taken at meetings or memos he has written to an interview. In one dispute we entered, an employee filed a fifteen-page grievance. This "position paper" was a key to understanding the depth of hurt and rejection he felt when his department was merged into another, larger department.

An interesting feature of secondary sources is that, for many conflict participants, the documents will tell the entire story, while, for the mediator, they are only a small piece of the puzzle. During a lengthy interview, the employee with the fifteen-page grievance said, "I overstated my case to get their attention." So, take secondary sources as indicators of the conflict rather than as accurate records of all you need to know. They are just one more useful source of information.

Each step taken in the Entry and Diagnostic stages helps to create the safety nets for mediation work. It can be a struggle to stay open long enough to allow a clear picture of the dispute to emerge, especially since most organizations demand "a quick fix." During entry and diagnosis, slow is best and haste does make waste. The trust built in carefully going through these stages will carry you through the rough water ahead.

Mediation Planning

With a fairly clear idea of the scope and issues of the dispute, it's time to make some key decisions about how to proceed with the actual mediation. There are five key questions to answer for yourself.

1. Who should be involved in the actual mediation?

Mediation is best conducted with the smallest number of people possible so there is maximum privacy, efficiency and flexibility. However, at times when organizational changes are pending or trust and openness are at issue, involving all key stakeholders is the best route to take. The mediator needs to decide about the scope of the mediation based on a full diagnosis.

Consider including the actual parties in the conflict as well as key decision makers about the issue at hand, anyone who can block the implementation of an agreement and those who are invested in the outcome of the conflict and are credible and trustworthy to the conflict parties. Any or all of those people may need to be in the actual mediation, depending on what configuration of people will assist in getting lasting agreements to benefit the interested parties.

You may not need all of these people present for the entire mediation process. Rather, you can decide what you need specifically from each person. For example, one person may need to be present only when a particular issue is discussed. Another may need to be present for the first fifteen minutes to give symbolic support and approval to the process. You could also obtain what you need from someone in a separate meeting before or during the mediation.

Whatever the judgment you make, there must be agreement on both the participants and the process before the mediation begins in order to prevent sabotage of agreements. For example, when some constituencies don't approve of an agreement, they can refuse to follow or implement it because they had not empowered the representative to decide for them. Such last ditch refusals often lower trust, create discouragement and entrench parties in their positions, hampering any future progress.

Particularly difficult is when critical parties will not come to the mediation table, often grinding collaborative efforts to a halt. In this case, you need to decide what you actually need from the party who refuses and if you can obtain it in any other way or from another source. In one multi-party dispute we mediated, a representative from a federal agency refused to be a part of the mediation, saying that he was not a part of the problem. In fact, other disputants needed information from his office and perhaps some decision making on his part that would affect larger issues. To sidestep his intransigence, we asked the state senator, a more powerful person, to obtain the information, either from this agency or from another source.

You also can proceed without the reluctant one, while being clear about the limits of the agreement without his/her participation. Reaching an agreement may be the impetus for the resistant party's participation in future negotiations: the reluctant party may want to get on the bandwagon in order to be seen as part of a successful agreement.

2. What are the interests of each party?

Interviewing and observing usually give you an idea of the key issues in the conflict even though some others will almost always emerge during the actual mediation. A beginning knowledge of what is at stake also allows you to separate the kinds of interests presented: content, relational and procedural.

3. What do the parties have in common?

As we discussed earlier, focusing on commonalities is critical for depolarizing the dispute, binding the parties together, helping them see they live in the same universe, with common concerns and goals. A focus on commonalities is most often the most productive way to begin a mediation and can lead the disputants to a common vision toward which to move.

4. What are the priority interests of the parties?

Planning an agenda requires making some estimate of which interests are most important to each party. You may want to go from easy, to medium, to hard issues; alternate issues of different intensity; or start with a hard one that you think the disputants can solve in order to build confidence in the process. Since most disputants start the conflict with some anxiety and often suspicion, the way you build the agenda may make or break their willingness to proceed. More information on agenda setting is provided in the next chapter, pages 120–123.

5. What is the current state of the parties?

Often those in conflict feel they have had a chance to vent during the interviews and are ready to move forward. At other times, they may need to tell their stories and have the others in the conflict hear the intensity of their feelings. When planning the mediation, consider whether additional venting may be needed, so you can plan the time and the ground rules to do it safely.

Reviewing the Mediation Wheel will help you align the methods, skills, personal qualities and rules that contribute to making an effective diagnosis.

APPLICATION

- A **Conflict Process Diagnostic Guide** to help you formulate questions for interviews and focus on specific issues during observation.

- An **Organizational Elements Diagnostic Guide** to help you understand the context and constraints of the dispute.

- A **Conflict Observation Sheet** to help you focus on issues as you observe conflict.

- An **Interest Observation Sheet** for tracking the specific interests in the conflict.

- A **Communication Observation Sheet** to help you pinpoint the kinds of communication that keep conflict constructive or destructive.

- An **Analysis and Planning Guide** to help you analyze your data and make key decisions about how to proceed with the mediation.

YARBROUGH
GROUP

Conflict Process
Diagnostic Guide

Here are general guidelines as well as actual questions that may be useful in diagnosing the process elements of a conflict.

I. Expressed struggle

1. What precipitated the conflict? What were the triggering events?

2. What is the history of the conflict — in terms of the ongoing relationship between the parties and important events in which the conflict is embedded?

3. Describe the other's behavior. How does it increase, maintain or decrease the conflict?

4. Describe your behavior. How does it increase, maintain or decrease the conflict? What could you do to change your behavior and alter the conflict?

II. Interdependent parties

1. What do the parties have in common — credibility, success of the project, values, goodwill for the team, etc.?

2. Who else cares about the outcome of the conflict? Directly or indirectly? How much power do they have in the situation?

3. Who else could be of assistance in resolving this conflict? Are there valued and respected others?

4. Who will bring pressure to bear if this conflict is not resolved?

5. How are you dependent on the other for what you need? Do you feel more dependent than you perceive the other to be?

6. What specifically do you depend on the other for? Is there any way to alter those tasks to change the dependency?

7. What is the typical contact you have with the other?

   ▸ Frequency

   ▸ Meetings

   ▸ Number and composition of people present

8. Is there a desire or way to alter the contact to change the conflict?

III. Goals and resources

1. What do you perceive you have lost or will lose by this conflict?

2. What do you think ought to be done? By the other party? By others who could change the situation? By the organization?

3. How would your concerns be addressed by those changes?

4. What goals or concerns do you have in common with the other party?

5. When do you work together that is satisfactory and productive? What makes those instances different?

6. Do you feel like you can influence the other person? In what ways? On what issues?

7. In what ways, or on what issues, does the other influence you? Is that okay with you?

8. What will happen to you and the other(s) if you continue what you are now doing? Is that outcome preferable to settling with the other, knowing you will have to change some of what you want?

9. What are the payoffs for keeping the conflict just as it is? (Even in a destructive conflict, there are rewards that keep the conflict going. Such things as predictability, feeling superior to others or proving you cannot work with a certain person can be rewards.)

IV.   Interference

1. How, specifically, does the other interfere with you in what you need to get done?

2. Is it actual interference? Or a lack of support?

V.   Protection and planning

1. What do you need to feel okay about proceeding? Assurances? Coaching? More information? Conditions for protection and safety?

2. Are you willing to talk with the other about possible solutions that benefit you both? Are you aware that some of your behavior will likely have to change?

YARBROUGH
GROUP

Organizational Elements
Diagnostic Guide

I.   Organizational culture

1. What conflict behavior is supported and sanctioned by the culture?

2. Are there spoken, healthy norms for managing conflict?

3. What is the history of the organization, especially in relation to the founder? What kind of historical norms have there been for managing conflict that may have a grip on current conflicts?

II.   Structure of work

1. What are the roles, responsibilities and reporting relationships of the parties in conflict?

2. Are there inherent conflicts in the structure that masquerade as interpersonal conflicts?

3. Could anyone be in the roles in question and still be having a conflict? If so, is the intervention about role clarification and change, rather than about regulating the interpersonal aspect of the conflict?

III. Third-party representation

1. Is either party representing another group that constrains his/her choices?

2. Must there be a certain kind of public display to satisfy the group?

3. Can the mediation be set in a place that decreases the pressure of the group?

4. What concessions must be made to satisfy the group(s) represented?

IV. Leadership — positive and negative

1. Does the leadership model constructive conflict and does it support mediated conflict?

2. Are there interested third parties inside the organization who have the skills for mediation?

3. Are there heroes and heroines in the organization, past and present, to serve as reminders of constructive conflict?

4. Can peer or public opinion be used to move the conflict forward?

V. Reward structures

1. Do organizational rewards support constructive conflict?

2. What response do the parties anticipate if they manage this conflict constructively?

3. Can rewards be instituted that increase the likelihood of constructive conflict?

VI. Conflict management procedures

1. What informal and formal procedures exist currently for managing conflicts?

2. Are they used? With what impact?

3. How costly do disputants perceive the procedure to be in terms of time and money, reputation, image and impact on their work?

4. Do the people managing the procedures have skills for constructive conflict?

5. Do new procedures need to be instituted?

VII. Economic and cultural environment

1. What are the attitudes of the community in which the organization exists that support constructive or competitive conflict resolution?

2. How do the disputants desire to be seen by their constituencies? Board? Community? Does this have a bearing on how the conflict is being and can be handled?

YARBROUGH
GROUP

Conflict
Observation Sheet

	Not True				Very True
1. Conflicts and disagreements are encouraged and openly expressed. Examples:	1	2	3	4	5
2. Group members are willing to confront each other. Examples:	1	2	3	4	5
3. Group members receive critical comments non-defensively. Examples:	1	2	3	4	5

4. Interests rather than   1   2   3   4   5
    positions are discussed.
Examples:

5. Conflict strategies in
    this group/session are:

    a. Avoidance (smooth-   1   2   3   4   5
        ing, ignoring, denial).

    b. Maintenance (letting   1   2   3   4   5
        it percolate a while).

    c. Escalation (increas-   1   2   3   4   5
        ing the issues
        and/or urgency).

    d. De-escalation   1   2   3   4   5
        (searching for com-
        mon ground and
        creative alternatives).
Examples:

6. What are the major conflicts in this group/meeting?
Examples:

YARBROUGH
GROUP

Interest Observation Sheet

	Name	Name
Content Interests		
Relational Interests		
Procedural Interests		
Interests in Common		

YARBROUGH
GROUP

Communication
Observation Sheet

	Not True			Very True	

1. Communication is open   1   2   3   4   5
    (owned, target-identified,
    risk-involved, e.g., "I am
    concerned about you,
    Joe, when you look dis-
    gruntled" versus "People
    seem disgruntled here").
Examples:

2. Questions are used to   1   2   3   4   5
    gather information rather
    than make statements or
    to entrap.
Examples:

3. Communication is congru-   1   2   3   4   5
    ent (words and non-
    verbals match).
Examples:

4. Communication is   1   2   3   4   5
    affirming (people are
    acknowledged,
    encouraged, supported).
    Examples:

5. Group members   1   2   3   4   5
    express their feelings
    in the group (note
    which feelings are
    expressed and which
    ones go unexpressed).
    Examples:

6. Non-verbal messages   1   2   3   4   5
    reflect involvement in
    the interaction.
    Examples:

7. Physical indicators   1   2   3   4   5
    support goals of the
    group (space, touch,
    furniture, etc.).
    Examples:

8. What are some patterns of communication (e.g., how people maintain
    destructive or constructive sequences)?

YARBROUGH
GROUP

Analysis and Planning Guide

After collecting information, in order to devise a plan for mediation, you need to analyze the data and make some key decisions about how to proceed.

1. Who should be in the actual mediation? Consider:
   - ☐ Parties involved in the actual conflict.

   - ☐ Decision makers about the issue at hand.

   - ☐ Anyone who can block the implementation of an agreement.

   - ☐ Those who are invested in the outcome and are credible and trustworthy to the parties.

   - ☐ Stakeholders in the systems issues.

2. What are the interests of each party?
   - ☐ Content

   - ☐ Relational

   - ☐ Procedural

3. What do they have in common?

4. Order interests from most to least important for
              Party A   Party B

5. Based on these priorities, what will you start with? (You can go
    from easy, to medium, to hard issues; alternate issues of different
    intensity; or start with a hard one that you think the disputants
    can solve and hence build confidence in the process.)

6. What is the current state of the parties? Do they need venting time and a chance to repeat their stories? Or are they ready to proceed given your summary of the information?

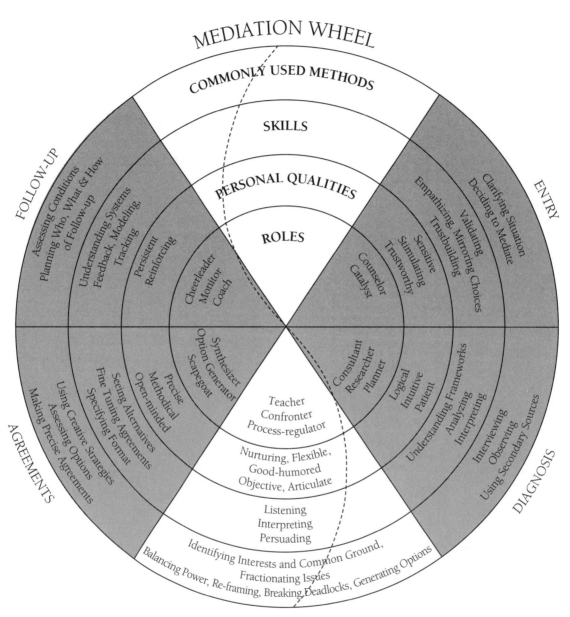

MEDIATION WHEEL

COMMONLY USED METHODS

SKILLS

PERSONAL QUALITIES

ROLES

FOLLOW-UP

ENTRY

DIAGNOSIS

NEGOTIATION

AGREEMENTS

Assessing Conditions
Planning Who, What & How
of Follow-up

Understanding Systems
Feedback, Modeling,
Tracking

Persistent
Reinforcing

Cheerleader
Monitor
Coach

Synthesizer
Option Generator
Scapegoat

Precise
Methodical
Open-minded

Seeing Alternatives
Fine Tuning Agreements
Specifying Format

Using Creative Strategies
Assessing Options
Making Precise Agreements

Teacher
Confronter
Process-regulator

Nurturing, Flexible,
Good-humored
Objective, Articulate

Listening
Interpreting
Persuading

Identifying Interests and Common Ground,
Fractionating Issues
Balancing Power, Re-framing, Breaking Deadlocks, Generating Options

Consultant
Researcher
Planner

Logical
Intuitive
Patient

Understanding Frameworks
Analyzing
Interpreting

Interviewing
Observing
Using Secondary Sources

Counselor
Catalyst

Sensitive
Stimulating
Trustworthy

Empathizing, Mirroring Choices
Validating
Trustbuilding

Clarifying Situation
Deciding to Mediate

CHAPTER

MEDIATION STAGE III: NEGOTIATION

M ANY PEOPLE THINK MEDIATION IS SYNONYMOUS WITH NEGOTIATION when in fact, negotiation is only one phase of the process. Creating a safe setting during entry and diagnosing the issues accurately are critical to the success of negotiation, the third stage of mediation. During the negotiation stage, you assist the parties in moving toward a mutually beneficial agreement. This is where you begin to combine the soft and hard skills presented on the Mediation Wheel, moving from simply listening to interpreting information and persuading the parties to move forward. To make the process as productive as possible, we will first focus on choosing and regulating the setting, then detail several key skills to guide disputants toward agreement. But first it is important to consider the physical aspects of the setting chosen for the work.

The Setting

A skilled mediator knows how to use the setting itself to facilitate settling the dispute. Consider the following elements:

Does the setting neutralize the hostility?

It is counterproductive to seat people in "opposition" positions — directly across the table from one another. Instead, place them side by side.

Figure 4

A productive setting for placing two protagonists, one mediator and a blackboard. Angling their chairs toward the mediator and a blackboard or flip chart focuses their attention on the problem rather than on the opponent.

Does the setting provide psychological support?

If participants are asked to meet in an office where one of them has been belittled or attacked, that setting will most likely prove counterproductive. Similarly, if the participants require confidentiality, they need to meet where they have privacy and where their comings and goings cannot be seen or heard by others. When a dispute has embroiled an entire office, the mediating participants should not have to walk through other offices after interviews or negotiations. Ask yourself as well as the conflict parties if there is anything about the physical arrangements that produces any uneasiness, then work to reduce or eliminate any problems.

Does the setting signal balanced power?

It is critical for the setting not to reinforce a power imbalance. Thus, it is best to have the parties meet in some neutral place, not in a location "owned" by either one. If you must meet on someone's home turf, choose that of the person with lower power. (This presumes that you have already talked with the parties about their reactions to the choice of setting.) Avoid increasing any perceived power discrepancy which, at a minimum, means not meeting in space controlled by the person with higher power.

Does the setting symbolize good faith?

Picking a neutral location reinforces the idea that all participants are here in good faith to bargain together. Choosing a neutral space, setting and honoring time limits, specifying ground rules and other process agreements are all ways to support effective negotiation. When the participants see that serious negotiation will commence, it will help them achieve their interests.

Skills that Provide the Keys to Success

The general flow of negotiation includes introducing the mediation, setting common ground and establishing the agenda. Throughout the process, you de-escalate hostility, continue to identify interests, constantly re-frame and fractionate issues and continue to generate options while moving toward agreement.

You will find that you need to reinforce the common ground throughout the conflict and continuously refine the underlying interests. While hostility is likely at the beginning, remember that it can also emerge at any moment in the conflict. You may also discover that the agenda you originally thought would serve to move participants forward must be rethought and reformatted.

Introducing the mediation

When introducing the session, you should repeat the purpose of the mediation, indicate your hope for resolution, highlight your stake and role in the outcome and remind parties of safety measures — confidentiality, no reprisals and the mediator's control of the

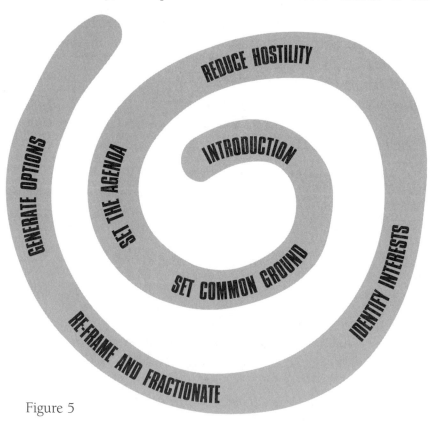

Figure 5

Weaving these skills together is more like a spiral than a straight line, although presenting this information on the printed page is necessarily linear. While there are many subtleties embedded in these steps, the basic outline provides a pattern to follow as you move through the negotiations.

process. Reinforce the parties' interdependence, affirm their willingness to meet and negotiate the conflict and acknowledge any strong feelings they may have as you prepare to preview the mediation process.

When participants are given detailed information and a positive framework for the session, it helps to put them at ease and predisposes them to deal productively with each other.

A sample introduction might sound like this:

> Thank you both for coming. I know it is difficult for both of you to take time out of your schedules when you are under so much pressure, but I know both of you are tired of spinning your wheels — an image you both used — trying to get your jobs done when you have to rely so much on each other.
>
> From what you have told me in the individual interviews, you have a great many things in common. It seems like these could be accomplished more effectively and with less irritation if you clarify your goals and decide how you want to reach them. I see so much overlap in your goals and believe you when you say you are ready to work on these issues, so I have great hope for resolution.
>
> I know there is a long history to this situation that has produced strong feelings. There will be time to acknowledge those and discuss what each of you can do by yourself and what we can do together to let go of the past feelings so there is room to solve current problems and begin to create more positive feelings.
>
> We have agreed that what we say here is confidential and that we will decide at the end of the mediation what will be reported to your boss. If we are successful, which I assume we will be, the actual decision will be reported. He only asks that your agreement not violate the project parameters. Other than that, you may decide how you will solve the issues. If for some reason you are not able to reach agreement, that fact will be reported. As I think you both are aware, that result would mean that your boss will mandate a decision and you would lose project flexibility and likely some credibility.
>
> As a Human Resources representative, I am here to assist with the process, not to direct what you decide. Since I know all the people involved, I will help you test the feasibility of some of your proposed solutions. I want this to work for you since you both are such valuable employees here.

The overall process will begin with setting the ground rules to insure that effective communication takes place, then to list the concerns and issues that you both have. Together we will prioritize the issues and decide how to approach them, generate as many ways as possible to meet your interests, reach agreement on the solution(s) best for both of you and decide on ways to reinforce and monitor the agreement so you don't have to repeat this negative cycle again.

As I indicated earlier, I may talk to each of you individually again if needed. If so, the same guidelines apply as when we had the individual interviews.

Are there any questions about the process or any of our roles?

Establishing common ground

Establishing commonalities begins to bind participants cooperatively when they thought they were connected only competitively.

Ground rules

One productive technique to begin establishing common ground is to get participants involved in setting the ground rules that form their operating agreement. By cooperating in agreeing on the ground rules, they begin with reaching a symbolic agreement which helps them become more committed to the entire process.

Ground rules have to do with how the parties will conduct themselves in the conflict to transform a negative dispute into a constructive one. Ground rules provide the boundaries to assure participants that negative conflict spirals will be contained.

As they are agreed upon, ground rules should be clearly announced, written down, distributed and enforced. We generally elicit the ground rules from participants at the beginning of the negotiation and write them on chart paper which is kept on the wall during the sessions. In addition, we have the ground rules typed and distributed to participants for reference throughout the mediation. We tell the parties that we take the ground rules seriously and consider them a contract among us for the duration of the mediation.

Typical ground rules for a mediation session might be:

► Only one person talks at a time.

► No interruptions are allowed.

► There will be equal talk time for all.

► There will be no name-calling.

► Criticisms will be translated into requests.

► All agreements will be examined many times and thought through before they are finalized.

► There will be confidentiality of the process and all individual concerns will be honored.

► There is an assurance of no reprisals in performance reviews.

► We agree that individual caucuses will be used when deemed necessary by the mediator or requested by either party.

► We will mutually agree on including any other people in the mediation before they are asked.

► We agree that Human Resources makes all logistical arrangements. If there is any dispute about those, we will discuss that openly and reach an agreeable solution.

► We will agree on the time and place to announce our agreement and will decide specifically on what role each will play in that announcement.

► Enough time will be committed to finish the agreement or a mutually acceptable deadline will be honored. (Deadlines may be determined by external events such as a specific City Council meeting, a tax or grant deadline, a product release date, etc.)

One incident dramatically underscored the importance of the mediator clearly enforcing ground rules. In an intense dispute, two people had repeatedly filed charges against one another with a social service agency alleging child abuse and neglect. In their third meeting, one person kept saying, "She is just crazy, that's all!" The other person did not respond and showed no evidence of being bothered by the name-calling. In fact, by the end of their session, they developed an agreement addressing all the major issues between them. The next day, however, the one who had been called "crazy" confronted the mediator: "You let her call me names. I will not pay money to be abused by her anymore. The agreement is off and I will not mediate anymore."

Ground rules must be enforced, even when ignoring them may appear to be tolerated. Otherwise, participants may later cite a broken ground rule as their reason for breaking agreements if they feel coerced or betrayed.

Enforcing ground rules can even provide some fun. Nine physician business partners all kept interrupting each other, in spite of the mediator's requests. To the next session, the mediator brought a "talking stick" — in this case, a flute from Nepal — to be passed to the person whose turn it was to speak. When someone would start to interrupt, the mediator would caution, "Careful, now. The flute is getting upset." Toward the end of the session, almost all the interruptions disappeared. When one participant would appear ready to interrupt, another would simply point to the flute. Silence would reign until the designated speaker resumed.

A final story to illustrate the importance of ground rules. Members of a city department were in a dispute about how to enforce city ordinances. One man, whose power resided in his ability to sidetrack any conversation, kept interrupting any movement toward agreement by two other employees. When the mediator called for a separate caucus between the two, the disrupter loudly proclaimed that we could not do that. By invoking the ground rules agreed upon, we were able to meet in an individual caucus, sidestep his interruptions, and move toward agreement. What may have seemed like a simple, common-sense statement about caucuses at the outset later become the ground upon which a constructive agreement was reached.

A special note about caucuses. Over the years, we have found private caucuses enormously helpful and now begin negotiation sessions by explaining that they are a mechanism used to clarify issues, to stop blaming and attacking, if necessary, and to provide a safety net for all concerned. Participants can also request private caucuses — either with or without the mediator — if they want to talk to their own group members.

We advise letting participants know that caucuses are a legitimate tool that you will use when you deem necessary, and one that they can use as well. The use of caucuses also requires ground rules, so spell them out. Tell participants that you will not make secret deals in a caucus and that you will maintain confidentiality about what you have been told in a caucus. Caucus information brought into the mediation session should first be agreed upon by the caucus session participants.

Conflict Issues

Listing the conflict issues that emerge in the diagnostic phase often provides an eye-opening experience. Disputants begin by thinking of themselves as diametrically opposed to everything the other stands for. Yet, when the issues are listed, they often see the commonalities they share.

These were the common issues that emerged in one session:

- Getting the job done.

- Stopping the backbiting.

- Wanting the conflict resolved.

- Not wanting to be seen as the only one causing a problem.

Common issues can involve overall goals, procedures, values, long-term success or even common enemies.

At a minimum, the conflict parties always share a common frustration with events and a feeling that the conflict is hindering them in some way. They are in it together — a common interest that's too often unacknowledged. No commonality is too small to acknowledge, even if it is only being willing to come to the bargaining table together.

Destructive moves

In an intense conflict, the parties have to stop engaging in counterproductive behavior before they can move forward. An important set of commonalities, then, involves an agreement to end such things as gossiping, going around the other, involving other people in the dispute, writing nasty memos, saying unpleasant things in meetings or talking to the media about the dispute. People doing destructive things will almost invariably say, "He made me do it," but they often appreciate the voluntary restraints that lessen toxic interactions and grow relieved when they can once again show their positive, productive sides.

Setting the agenda

After the hard work of diagnosis, agenda setting may seem a minor concern. However, it has been our experience that framing and ordering the agenda set the stage for transforming negative conflict into a productive experience. Parties in a dispute are often in disarray — frustrated, angry, linking issues, globalizing concerns about the other. Setting an agenda structures the interaction so you (and they) can proceed in an orderly fashion and not simply wander through issues as they pop up. Agenda setting also reassures participants that all their concerns will be heard, that all have an equal chance to influence what issues are discussed and that all issues are legitimate.

With a well-crafted agenda, participants begin to see possibilities that had previously been hidden. Agreeing on priorities begins the process of cooperation that disputes had undermined.

Mediators can approach the task of setting agendas in a variety of ways. Here are several options.[1]

An **ad hoc** agenda emerges as each party suggests an item and it is discussed in turn. A **simple agenda**, where the mediator lists items before the mediation and then proceeds one item at a time, is a somewhat more structured agenda.

Alternating choices lets each person take a turn choosing a topic. It is useful to begin this sort of agenda setting by saying something like, "Let's get all the concerns on the table, taking one from Sarah and then one from Steve, until we have them all." This process of taking turns can also work with a larger group by setting up sub-groups to meet and report back to the larger group.

Either the mediator or the participants can then rank the order of importance of the agenda items. Beginning with easier, smaller items first gives participants a chance to cooperate and negotiate, building up a bit of optimism about the process before they head into the more difficult, intensely disputed items.

To help participants rank order items, the mediator looks at each disputant's list of concerns and then asks each one which item they prefer to deal with first. The resulting list then forms the agenda.

With multiple parties and many issues, the list can be long enough to be daunting. Sometimes you can link priorities and show the participants how they can deal with them together. One person's priority might be to increase trust among team members, another may want to increase credibility with the boss while a third person might want to make the grant deadline. Then, the mediator might ask, "Could we increase credibility by meeting the deadline? And can we practice communication, as described in our ground rules, to enhance the trust as we work on this task?"

Combining issues may work. Or the participants may decide they have to deal directly with past violations of trust and ways to build trust anew before they can proceed to more substantive problem solving.

The *principled agenda* is a process that works when the parties can agree on abstract goals and then negotiate over the procedures of how to obtain the goals. In one conflict, two warring teams agreed that inter-departmental cooperation must be improved. The agreement needed to specify how. In another conflict, a top management team agreed on beginning a total quality process within the next year, agreed that they would all cooperate to do so and agreed that the design and delivery should be within a certain budget. The negotiation centered on how to establish the quality process, who would spearhead it and in what way.

Some conflicts are complex, and it is difficult to know what issues to begin with, since agreement on one issue would change another. This requires creating a *contingent agenda*. For instance, team members might need to deal with relational issues of respect or trust before they can decide about issues like applying for a team award. Negotiation over the degree of interdependence of a cross-functional team would most likely precede discussions of how to structure the interactions of a newly formed team.

With a contingent agenda, you can agree that a solution on each item is tentative so that, if the best solution to one item affects a previous one, the negotiators can cycle back to an earlier decision and refine it. This sort of process can prevent or break deadlocks because it acknowledges the interlocking relationship of the issues. Issues can be linked so that concessions on one issue are traded for concessions on another. Since disputants often will not settle on one issue for fear they will lose leverage on another, a contingent agenda avoids such potential deadlocks.

This agenda strategy lends itself to a "how-to" approach. Creating "how-to" sentences also helps disputants package the issues to indicate a direction for resolution. For example, "How can we maintain the aesthetic values of the city while completing the building project?" Sub-issues might be size and height of the building, amount of land for open space and landscaping. The general statement, however, presumes agreement on the principle of aesthetics and on the completion of the building, thus establishing common ground.

Members of a hospital intensive care unit listed a "low census" as a major issue. The low patient census resulted in fluctuating staffing problems, which in turn created conflict among the nurses. One "how-to" statement offered was "How do we create more major accidents to increase our critical care patients?" That met with laughter, even though it hit on an underlying assumption — the unit, as currently defined, stayed in business as long as there were critically injured patients. Rethinking their focus on the number of patients, they then asked, "How can we expand our mission to take into account current trends in the emergency health care field and thus stabilize our staffing?" The group began to move from short-term to long-term planning and to becoming proactive instead of simply responding to changes.

After a thorough diagnosis, a mediator decides to set the agenda or to have those in the conflict work together on setting it. This is a judgment call and the choice should hinge on the impact either option will have on the conflict. In one multi-party conflict, one disputant kept wondering when all the parties would set the agenda. Frustrations were so high that involving the parties in deciding how to group the issues would have both stalled the dispute and increased the tension. The mediator chose to frame the agenda, hoping the negotiation could begin on a positive note. The disputants accepted the framing, and the discussion began.

De-escalating anger, attack and hostility

One reason for conflicts is that people get frustrated by not getting their needs met and often attack one another. Anger can erupt in any mediation session without a moment's notice. We have seen calm, rational business people suddenly jump out of their chairs and shout at others in the midst of a session. We also have seen seething anger expressed in controlled, seemingly rational ways as the disputants inflicted painful psychological damage on one another.

Telling people not to be angry does not help. Mediators and disputants need productive ways both to acknowledge and to de-escalate anger so that all parties' interests can be explored. The following tactics can help when tempers flare at any stage in the negotiations. Please note that these tactics are not listed in any particular order and are offered as a tool kit with which to work. If one tactic does not work, try another. The goal is to transform the anger to energy used for the benefit of the disputants.

Seek more information

Anger can come from feeling unheard and people often exaggerate and generalize their statements in order to get through to the other party. Asking for more information shows that they have been heard and that you seek to understand more precisely what issues are of concern. You can seek more information by asking about specifics, guessing about specifics or paraphrasing the speaker's ideas.

Often you'll hear an angry person exclaim, "Sometimes I think you don't take me seriously. It seems that everything I say goes in one ear and out the other." Consider these options:

- *Ask about specifics.* "I'd understand what you mean better if you could give me some examples of when you feel ignored."

- *Guess about specifics.* "Are you talking about last week when Gene went ahead and sent that report out, after you asked him not to?"

- *Paraphrase.* "It sounds like you're mad at Gene because you think he's just humoring you or something. Is that it?"

- *Agree with the speaker.* Often people stay angry because the other person is refusing to acknowledge the truth of any part of their statement or refusing to own any part of the problem. Agreeing with certain parts of a statement, specific facts or perceptions, and admitting error, can de-escalate the conflict. To return to the same angry person described above:

- *Agree with facts.* "I have noticed that when Gene is tired and preoccupied, his attention wavers. Is that your experience, Gene?"

- *Agree with perceptions.* "I can see from your point of view it might seem that way. Gene has said he is not expressive and gets even less expressive when his position has not been heard."

▸ *Admit error:* "I heard Gene say that he does do what you say. Do you need to hear that again or in some other way?"

Make reassuring comments

In most conflicts, people are afraid of losing something important, even the relationship that is conflictual. Fear is often expressed as anger — acting boisterously, pushing, name-calling, blaming or sulking — making it difficult to know people need reassurance. If this is the case, it is helpful for the mediator to make reassuring comments, or to assist the disputants in doing so, to reduce their fear and thus their anger.

Reassuring comments could include:

▸ How hopeful you are that this can be worked out.

▸ That you understand the relationship is important and know that both parties want to maintain it.

▸ That you understand their fears and will work to make the mediation as safe as possible.

▸ That both sides are likely to have to adjust to different ways of doing things but that, in your experience, making those adjustments involves less frustration than they are experiencing in the conflict situation.

Reassuring comments need to be honest, not simply empty words. When given congruently, reassurances can shift the entire tone of the discussion in a more positive direction.

Take the role of the disputants

This usually increases your own understanding as well as the other's feeling of being understood. You can say, "I see what you mean. If I had been treated in a way that I saw as unfair, I wouldn't cooperate either."

Asking them to take the role of the other party can also help each to see the other's position. You might ask:

▸ What do you think will happen to Fran if she does what you ask?

> ▸ What would you do in her position?

> ▸ What do you think Fran thinks?

Slow down the process

Conflicts can create destruction because each person feels out of control and the "runaway," out-of-control feeling stimulates their fears. Just slowing the pace can calm people down enough to defuse a situation.

Some simple ways to slow down the process include:

▸ Talking more slowly.

▸ Waiting longer before responding.

▸ Taking time-outs for breaks.

▸ Waiting for a day or a week.

▸ Taking time to write down what the other person is saying slows the pace and demonstrates a commitment to accuracy.

Control the process productively

You can arrange the physical surroundings to help maximize collaboration. You can set and repeat the ground rules for greater safety. By helping defuse anger and turn the energy into productive problem-solving behaviors, you begin to help participants save face. By allowing them strong emotions while helping channel the emotions positively, you help make the conflict constructive. Frightened people are not good at negotiating.

Identifying interests

People are in conflict because they want something; they have some interest or need they are trying to fulfill. The usual way disputants identify their interests is through a particular position, such as, "I want $3,000 for the car."

People take positions as a way to manage the conflict while trying to meet their *underlying interests*. Underlying the demand for a certain price for a car could be the need for resources — money for a down payment on another car — or could signal an interest in fairness: "I would rather take nothing than be ripped off when I have taken such good care of this car."

"I want production to increase by 10 percent," the manager declares. Underlying this position could be an interest in maintaining one's status and reputation in the organization, the need to live up to a quality agreement or even the need to hold a team accountable.

"I want a promotion to Vice President," says the researcher. Here the underlying demand could be a need to be successful, to be better than someone else or to be in a position to work on a favorite project.

Positions, once taken, tend to harden and become the focus for the dispute. The parties actually lose sight of their underlying interests, and the conflict spirals into a tug-of-positions with each party not wanting to lose.

If the disputants stick on position, then there are only three possible outcomes of the conflict:

- ▸ Someone wins and the other loses.

- ▸ Both lose.

- ▸ There is a compromise, splitting the differences.

In all three outcomes, the underlying interests generally go unmet.

Paradoxically, taking a position keeps people from getting to their real, underlying interests. The researcher does not get a promotion, nor are any other means explored for signalling that the person is valued. The manager compromises by only increasing production quotas by 5 percent, but ways of improving the quality contract are not explored, since that issue was not uncovered.

When you examine the real, underlying interests, it's easy to see that there are multiple ways of meeting those interests, other than the position proposed. And that is the point. Mediation is a powerful tool largely because the mediator focuses on the underlying interests, not positions, in order to find multiple solutions to problems.

In *Getting to Yes*, Roger Fisher and William Ury identify the differences between positions and interests. What they don't address, however, is how to identify these underlying interests. Commanding one to find the interest behind the position does not offer a process you can use.

We have had success in helping participants identify interests using the following process. Earlier, we discussed three kinds of goals or interests: (1) content, (2) relational and (3) procedural. Content interests are the typical objective factors such as salary, promotions, wanting a fair bargain or a good return on an investment, adequate compensation for your contribution to a project, being paid what you are worth. Relational interests center on the relationship between people — their interpersonal needs for inclusion, power, affection, respect, recognition, security, esteem and self-actualization. Procedural interests center on how things are to be accomplished.

Almost without exception, when a dispute first arises, it is expressed in terms of content or procedural issues. And those content and procedural issues are usually stated in terms of a position, a way of solving as-yet-unnamed underlying issues.

Let's return to the case of the two business partners who began mediation with one asking for $30,000 — a content position. During private sessions, it became clear that Sam felt his former friend had excluded him — a relational interest. He was hurt by being excluded. But, unaccustomed to saying, "You hurt my feelings and I don't want to be your best friend anymore," Sam instead asked for $30,000 to compensate him for his "business contribution" to the partnership.

Paradoxically, people who get the "content" they want are still not satisfied. Just talk to someone who won a court battle. They often declare, "Yes, I got the money, but I still hate the bastards!"

Identifying the interests, we believe, is a key to managing conflicts successfully, since solutions need to meet underlying interests.

It's important to remember two important things about identifying underlying interests. First, as we noted above, people often are confused about what their interests are, and, second, conflict parties almost always have multiple interests. The mediator's task is to help the people in dispute discover the interests that propelled them into the conflict. Then, once you recognize what the underlying interests are, remember that there are always multiple solutions that can meet those interests.

Earlier, we discussed how to interview disputants, how to observe them and how to diagnose their interests. But remember that interests usually will need to be clarified as the negotiation progresses. Often new interests will emerge as well.

You can clarify interests by asking:

- What if? If he or she were to apologize, what would that give you?
- What will it take? What will it take for you to cooperate?
- Why not? Why won't you cooperate? What is in your way?
- What would be the perfect situation?
- How would you like to be treated?
- What problem(s) are we trying to solve?
- What is your goal?
- What concerns you the most?
- When are you irritated? Most satisfied?
- Describe a situation when things went well.
- What do you want? What would it mean if you got it?
- What are two other ways you can get what you want?
- Can you tell me why you feel so strongly about this?
- Before this conflict started, what did you want?
- What would help you feel good?
- How do you want to be treated by him or her?

By using open-ended questions, the mediator gets the opportunity to listen for the underlying interests. The next step is articulating those interests for the disputants. So, if one disputant says, "I am most irritated when he rushes into my office and demands that I listen," the mediator might respond by saying, "It sounds like you would like him to show you respect, either by letting you know when he is coming or by making an appointment with you."

In one legal conflict, the defendant's lawyers offered the cash settlement the plaintiff requested in out-of-court negotiations. But the plaintiff quite vehemently refused the offer. Often in such situations, the response is a variation of the question-cum-accusation, "What do you mean, you won't take the money? That's what you've been demanding all along." At this key moment, however, with some coaching, the lawyer, instead of taking the usual path of blaming the plaintiff for being stubborn and recalcitrant, chose to probe for the underlying interest.

"Why not?" the lawyer asked simply. The plaintiff replied, "Because no one has apologized for the inconvenience of this whole proceeding" — a comment that signalled a strong relational interest that had more meaning than the money. Listening to this conflict from an interest perspective, the next logical question is, "Who needs to apologize to you, in what way, for you to be satisfied?"

Often, disputants can't tell you their interests because they don't know what they are. Or they won't tell you, perhaps because it is not safe for them to do so, or perhaps because they feel embarrassed, especially if their feelings don't fit their self image — it's not okay for a hard-nosed businessman to want to feel included, for example. Some feelings are simply not allowed in certain organizational cultures. If people have previously been taken advantage of, belittled or betrayed when they were direct and spoke freely, they will be reluctant to speak out again. Fearing they will lose face in some other way may also keep them from saying what their interests are.

Here's an example from one mediation (see pages 146–158):

	George	Angela
Content Interests	Video completion and successful group. Time in a video lab.	Have the video done and have a successful group.
Relational Interests	Politics, not to have to play them, to stay out of the game. Flexibility with others. Fear of losing his job. Image as an "action person." Being a creative person in eyes of others and self. Commitment to the job. Influence (and power) as a player.	Be a team player (and seen as one). Have respect of others (politics, linkages in the organization are important). Being viewed as competent on the job. Family is important — juggling family issues. Job perfection — doesn't want her job performance judged by family involvement. Be a model female employee (one of only two in the company at this level — worked her way up). Privacy, boundaries, not have to dredge up feelings.
Procedural Interests	Wants to "go with the flow" and not have a lot of hassle.	Structure, order, predictability in terms of procedures.
Issues in Common	**Both Want**	Influence. Videos — agree on their importance and completion. Jobs and security. Respect. Competence, perceived as doing a good job. Both value innovation and creativity. Both have the same boss and want to please him. Both have fears.

Thus, some underlying interests, especially relational ones, need to be identified by observing patterns in the dispute and hypothesizing about their nature. Here are some hints.

During your observations notice

Word choices. When Carl says, "I just want fairness," he is signalling a procedural issue. When Lindsey exclaims, "You are trying to control me!" she is indicating a relational interest of freedom and choice. People will almost invariably use some strong word expressing their underlying interest. Watch for key words such as compensation, reward, production, competence and treatment.

Triggering events. What happens prior to a conflict gives you clues about the underlying issues. If a conflict erupts among the staff after every board meeting, the conflict may be about the board itself and not what is being discussed by the staff. One work group routinely had conflicts roughly two weeks before the annual performance evaluations. What a hint!

Repetitive patterns. What are the patterns that get enacted over and over again? They can signal an underlying issue. Each time the supervisor visited the work site, employees verbally abused one another as soon as she left. What is the underlying issue?

Themes. Themes can emerge through the kinds of jokes and stories told, the kinds of images and metaphors that are repeated, the topics that generate the most energy or the ones that freeze the group. Sometimes risky conflict issues will emerge in more indirect ways. For example, when one group got close to underlying issues, they began telling stories about how those who make political mistakes do not recover in the organization. The mediator followed up by saying, "So, it sounds as if there is not enough safety here to proceed with these risky issues. What do we need to do to increase the protection so you don't suffer for doing this hard mediation work?" You can clarify the underlying concerns by verbalizing them.

Non-verbal cues. Tone of voice, body posture, eye contact and other body language can spotlight interests. Whenever there is some incongruence — such as a person saying pleasant words while frowning — the odds are that there are other issues in the conflict not being addressed. Non-verbal cues "leak out" a warning to be alert to unacknowledged interests. You may want to ask about what is going on for the person at that moment, or make some guesses, or intervene to solve the problem and watch for the Blip, the change, to see if the incongruity is resolved.

Indicators of position. Anytime anyone takes a position, be alert for an underlying interest. "More of . . . ," "less of . . . ," "to get . . . ," and "to have . . ." are phrases that often flag position statements.

Location of discussion. The discussion location gives clues about the level of interest. Examining one conflict revealed that the public relations issue was talked about in the committee meeting, the need for approval was hashed out in the parking lot and the need for influence was addressed only in phone conversations. The deeper interests were discussed in more private, protected surroundings, a hint about the difficulty of addressing those issues up front. If you can't decipher the underlying interests, especially relational ones, try asking people what they talk about in the parking lot or bathroom or over the phone to trusted others. Often, people start laughing when asked these kinds of questions. But then they begin to open up in private caucuses, if not in the negotiating session.

Which brings us to an important point about clarifying interests. Most interests do need to be articulated in the negotiation session. However, some do not have to be said straightforwardly or even mentioned in the negotiating session at all. Consider the person who has a high need to look good. Instead of putting that interest on the wall chart, the mediator might simply make a mental note of it and then make certain that whatever agreement is discussed includes ways for that person to maintain status. If another has high safety needs, the mediator need not say, "It sounds like you're scared and need a lot of protection." Instead, making many reassuring statements and offering protection may allow the frightened one to relax enough to be able to contribute to the negotiations.

Most people proceed along until something or someone steps in their way. When their path is blocked, they push to go through or around the obstacle. Once again, it is not that people won't talk about their underlying interests, but that most of the time they don't know themselves. Then someone — perhaps a mediator — comes along to help them clarify what is bothering them and to explore their choices. Remembering that both the mediator and the disputants are embarking on a journey to find and meet mutual needs is a perspective we find helps us to be patient.

Fractionating and re-framing issues

In most conflicts, issues tend to both expand and get lumped together. What begins as a one- or two-issue dispute expands to include more and more as people say something like, "Yes, I'm concerned about my promotion, but also about office morale, our lack of a strategic plan and the overall philosophy of the group." As the conflict intensifies, it swells into one huge, seemingly unmanageable lump of issues. Fractionating and re-framing are skills that can be crucial in clarifying interests, breaking them into manageable parts and articulating them so that they can be heard and addressed.

Fractionating

This process involves dividing the issues into manageable units and then generating ways of solving each individual unit. After each issue has been tentatively settled, it's then possible to see how each partial settlement affects the other issues.

Here are some sample approaches to help "un-clump" multiple issues:

- ▶ What part of the problem is most important to you right now?
- ▶ That is certainly an important related issue, but we will have better luck taking them one at a time. What was that first one again?

▶ Okay. Now we have many concerns on the table. We will go through them all. Let's start with the most straightforward ones first. Let's begin with job security.

▶ Whew! We have a bundle of issues before us. Can either of you see ways we can group these into three or four issues so we can take them one at a time?

The mediator can also fractionate process issues to move the conflict forward. For example, many people block their understanding of others' concerns by lumping together understanding and agreement. The mediator can help disputants separate the two by saying, "It seems like it's difficult for you to hear each other. I want to remind you that our first step is to clarify and understand the issues. Then, we will see where we agree and where we disagree and begin to work for a solution that benefits you both."

Re-framing

In most disputes, the language choices reflect habitual thought patterns that work against solving the dispute. Re-framing is a particularly effective technique for freeing the disputing parties from old patterns so they can move forward to resolution. Re-framing is effective when used on many levels, from recasting the language disputants use to redefining the nature of the dispute.

Language re-framing. Adversarial language can be avoided by referring to the conflict as "struggles" or "problems," positions as "viewpoints," the parties as "your group" and negotiations as "discussions."

One participant may ask why John "has to nitpick the agreement." Such a judgment-laden phrase needs to be re-framed to remove the negativity implicit in it. The mediator might respond by saying that John is going over the agreement with a fine-toothed comb to make sure there aren't any details that might cause future difficulties.

When business partners call one another "money hungry," the mediator can respond with, "They do want adequate compensation for their professional skills, don't they?"

Here are a few more examples for re-framing judgmental comments.

From: He is unprofessional.

To: He tries hard to balance a family life with work demands.
He wants to be rewarded for his work.
He's honest about the job not being the only thing in his life.

From: She is not a team player.

To: She is an independent thinker.
She seems really clear about what she wants.
She doesn't seem to have the same interest in making others
feel good that you do.

From: He is just blowing smoke; he didn't prepare those remarks.

To: He is really an intuitive, seat-of-the-pants kind of guy.
He is very good on his feet.
He thinks quickly in public.

From: He is inflexible.

To: He sure seems afraid of change.
He does seem more comfortable when the rules are clearly
known.
He has a way of taking a position and sticking to it.

From: She is arrogant.

To: She is quite self-assured.
She doesn't know how to give positive non-verbal cues to others
and, as a result, people see her as liking herself too much.
She must be used to being left out and has given up trying to
get in on social groupings.

From: She is selfish.

To: She knows how to get her needs met.
She is able to keep others from controlling her life.
She sure can keep herself going by never being depleted.

From: He is uncooperative.

To: There must be something causing him to pull back; usually he
is a very engaging guy.
The dispute between the two of you must have driven him to
giving up.
He hasn't yet developed the skill of giving positive feedback to
others.

Language re-framing helps to chip away at the concretized perceptions the parties develop of one another. It is very easy to keep a dispute going and justify all kinds of nasty countermoves if each party sees the other as all bad. On the other hand, it is difficult to keep a dispute at a high level of intensity when one begins to see the other in a more favorable, more human light.

One final note. You can also re-frame negative descriptions in terms of what the person can offer the organization. If, for example, Jim is accused of being rigid, you can note how his ability to be clear and decisive might be useful to the organization, which both re-frames and helps find a niche for the person's talents after the dispute is managed.

Re-framing positions into interests. When someone says, "I just want them to punch the time clock like everyone else," the challenge is to find the underlying interest. It might be uniformity, hours worked, control, sense of trust or some other issue. Re-framing, with participants actively involved in the process, helps clarify the underlying issue. The questions given to clarify interests, page 129, can be helpful here as well.

Re-framing specific goals into larger goals. This involves moving to a higher level of abstraction. For instance, two nation states that talk about "national security" can be moved to discuss "regional stability." Similarly, an organizational dispute that begins over who calls the shots can be re-framed into ways to keep both parties involved in the business decisions in a meaningful way.

A labor/management struggle over wages can be recast into a search for ways to continue to turn a profit while fairly compensating the employees. Moving to the next level, to superordinate goals, allows the parties to see their interdependence and see the problems as jointly shared.

Re-framing from independence to interdependence. A person's exclamation of isolation and frustration — "I'm so frustrated I can't get the job done" — can be re-framed to a statement of interdependence and connection: "So, you need a way to get Marcia to help you get the job done." Almost invariably, disputants in a conflict feel alone, as if they have to do most things by themselves, usually while contending with interference from others. Re-framing statements in a way that joins possibilities begins the process of seeing the world from a cooperative perspective.

Re-framing from complaints to requests. Most conflicts are fueled by each side complaining about the other and destructive conflicts stay at this level. Yet, implicit in attacks are requests for change. Moving from gripes to goals, from harangues to specific requests for action, allows the parties to begin negotiating about those requests rather than remaining stuck in an attack/defense cycle. The mediator could re-frame "He's a sexist," to "So, from what you've said, it sounds like you want higher visibility job assignments." Another might re-frame "He betrayed me by not supporting me in that project meeting," to "So, you need him to give you clearer expectations and more check-points during the project in order to get his support."

Re-framing complaints into requests is one way to identify what the person with the complaint wants the other person to do. It is helpful for the participants to clarify the nature of their requests as well, to be clear whether they are asking for information, for under-standing, for feelings or for actions.

Kinds of Requests:

- ▶ Information exchange. "I want you to hear information I have to offer you or I want information from you."

- ▶ "I want you to listen and understand."

- ▶ "I want you to feel a certain way" — sad, guilty, bad or happy.

- ▶ Action within the existing structure.
  "If we must operate within a matrix, how can we do that well?"

- ▶ Action to change the structure.
  "I want policies, procedures or organizational structures changed to reach our goals."

Generating options

As interests are clarified, you begin to notice that there are many ways to meet the needs of the conflict participants. Multiple ways of solving problems allow flexibility in the conflict, help people to move past win/lose solutions and also move the focus away from the people and onto the problems.

We'll outline several formats for generating options, beginning with the time-honored technique of brainstorming.[2]

Brainstorming helps generate options by withholding criticism. It is a two-step process that begins by asking for some possible solutions. Then each person contributes to the list of solutions without any analysis or criticism of the ideas. The goal is to generate as many solutions as possible and to get the creative juices flowing. Often the most bizarre suggestions will prove to have the most value.

Setting the stage for brainstorming

- *Define your purpose.* Think of what you would like to walk out of the meeting with.

- *Choose a few participants.* The group should be large enough for a stimulating interchange, yet small enough to encourage both individual participation and freewheeling inventing. Usually between five and eight people is optimum.

- *Change the environment.* Select a time and place to distinguish the brainstorming session from regular discussions. The more a brainstorming session differs from a normal meeting, the easier it is for participants to suspend judgment.

- *Design an informal atmosphere.* What does it take for you and others to relax? It may be talking over a drink, or meeting at a vacation lodge in some picturesque location, or simply taking off ties and jackets and using first names.

- *Choose a facilitator.* Someone needs to keep the meeting on track, to make sure everyone gets a chance to speak, to enforce any ground rules and to stimulate discussion by asking questions.

During brainstorming

- *Seat the participants side by side, facing the problem.* The physical reinforces the psychological. Physically sitting side by side reinforces the sense of coming together to tackle a common problem. When facing each other, people tend to respond personally and engage in dialogue or argument; seated in a semicircle facing a blackboard, people tend to respond to the problem in front of them.

  If the participants do not all know each other, begin with introductions all around, followed by clarification of the ground rules.

- *Clarify the ground rules, emphasizing that a ban on criticism is vital to the process.* You may want to consider adopting ground rules to make the entire session off the record or perhaps to refrain from attributing ideas to any individual participant.

- *Outlaw negative criticism of any kind.* We all invent only within the limits set by our working assumptions. But in the joint inventing of the brainstorming process new ideas can be created. If ideas are shot down unless they appeal to everybody, the implicit goal becomes coming up with an idea that no one will shoot down. Unless wild ideas are encouraged, even those that may lie well outside the realm of possibility, the group's creative thinking will drop to the lowest common denominator. Sometimes the most off-the-wall ideas provide a springboard for generating realistic ideas and options that no one would have considered before.

- *Brainstorm.* Once the purpose of the meeting and the ground rules are clear, let the group's imaginations go. Try to come up with a long list of ideas, approaching the question from every conceivable angle.

- *Record the ideas in full view.* Recording ideas on large sheets of newsprint hung around the room is beneficial in several ways: it gives the group a tangible sense of collective achievement; it reinforces the no-criticism rule; it reduces the tendency to repeat; and it helps stimulate even more ideas. But a blackboard will do in a pinch. Making the ideas visible is an important part of the process.

After brainstorming

- ▸ *Mark the most promising ideas.* Relax the no-criticism rule a bit in order to winnow out the most promising ideas. Star or color-code the ones that members of the group like best. This is still not the stage of deciding but merely nominating ideas worth developing further.

- ▸ *Invent improvements for promising ideas.* Take one promising idea and invent ways to make it better or more realistic. Create ways to carry it out. The task at this stage is to make the idea as attractive as possible. Soften any constructive criticism with positive information: "What I like best about that idea is . . ." or, "Might it be better if . . . ?"

Set up a time to evaluate ideas and decide. Before the group breaks up, draw up a selective and improved list of ideas from the session and set up a time for deciding which of these ideas to advance in your negotiations and how to best do that.

Brainstorming in sub-groups

In this variation on the brainstorming process, people are asked individually to write down all possible solutions. Then the larger group is divided into sub-groups. Each small group has a recorder who records all the options and each group makes certain that *all* suggestions are recorded. Even in two-person conflicts, the mediator can ask the people to get creative and generate a list of all possible solutions that are then placed on a board or flip chart.

Whenever there is a work group conflict, sub-group structures work well to generate options. The sub-groups brainstorm and then report back to the larger group. Downsizing the decision-making group helps get everyone involved, helps generate creative solutions and often provides some fun in the process. When people in the small groups begin breaking into laughter, they are relaxing, releasing tension and being creative.

Hypothetical plausible scenarios

Detailed possible scenarios are developed about how a problem can be solved. The group can be asked to imagine a perfect situation five or ten years in the future, for instance. Visioning exercises can often be useful here as well.

If the group is large enough to be subdivided, all the smaller groups need to be heard by the entire group. Plausible scenarios can reveal detailed looks at possible solutions. As scenarios are shared, some commonality often emerges among them. Common threads can be used to draw together and refine the scenarios before the advantages and disadvantages of each are examined.

Single text negotiating document

A single text is just what the name suggests. The mediator identifies all interests and stakeholders, then drafts a proposal that will satisfy a majority of interests and stakeholders. The draft is circulated among all participants for their comments and changes. As comments and changes are incorporated, the draft is recirculated until all parties agree.

Outside resources

Books, films, previous cases and other people's experiences can all suggest solutions. If neither the parties nor the mediator are able to generate creative solutions, other outside resources can expand everyone's thinking and bring fresh insight into the problem.

Assessing options

After generating many options, the disputants need to assess those options as they move toward agreement. At this stage, people can get confused, flustered or overwhelmed, especially if there are many options to consider. They may even revert to their old positions and argue for their original proposals. To prevent confusion or backsliding, help them consider which solutions will be most effective and satisfying.

Which options:

▸ Meet the interests of all parties?

▸ Meet the highest priority interests?

▸ Fall within an acceptable settlement range, where some key over-lapping interests are met?

▸ Will be supported by key stakeholders in the decision and/or will serve the larger organization?

▸ Are considered fair by all parties?

▸ Will be likely to endure, given the circumstances?

▸ Improve, or at least do not damage, ongoing relationships?

▸ Will be unlikely to set up future conflicts of the same sort or spin-offs of this conflict?

▸ Build credibility within the organization?

Underlying all these processes is a profoundly simple idea: the people are the source of their solutions. Imposing solutions does not work in the long term, and ignoring any of the parties in choosing solutions simply sets the stage for further conflict. These techniques are designed to help the parties create their own solutions — which then become solutions they will heed.

APPLICATION

▸ The **Negotiation Checklist** is an overall guide to what needs to be accomplished in Mediation Stage III.

▸ A **Sample Negotiation Dialogue** conveys the way skills weave and spiral throughout a negotiation and shows how to work with unexpected elements as they arise during the process of negotiation.

YARBROUGH
GROUP

Negotiation Checklist

Have you:

☐ Established a safe setting?

☐ Established common ground?

☐ Let parties vent if necessary?

☐ Established an agenda acceptable to all parties?

☐ Broken conflict into manageable parts?

☐ Framed the conflict in such a way that all understand what they can gain by cooperating and lose by competing?

☐ Balanced power between parties? Not let one dominate the other?

☐ Generated many options?

☐ Evaluated options with clear criteria?

☐ Made it clear that if they are stuck and refuse to move there are unpleasant consequences?

Sample Negotiation Dialogue

George and Angela, mentioned earlier, discuss different issues and show how a negotiation depends on the participant's views. This conversation also shows how to work with unexpected elements that may emerge during the process of negotiation.

The Context: A dispute between Angela, the longtime valued assistant to the president of a mid-sized video production company, and George, a newly hired producer, threatens to divide the small organization and imperils meeting an important deadline. The president called in a mediator who has already met with both parties separately before this conversation took place.

Mediator: *Hi, Angela. Thank you for coming. I appreciate you putting this into your schedule. I found the interview with you very helpful and informative.*

Angela: I like to be helpful.

Mediator: *You were very helpful, thank you. And, George, I really appreciate the fact that you came here today, especially since you are feeling all this pressure about getting the video done. I think it's important for the two of you to realize that you are cooperating to try and solve the problem. That's step one.*
In the first interviews, we talked about the issues for you and I asked each of you to think about what you need from the other person to help you get back to doing your job the way you would like to. Do you both recall that?

Angela: I'm sorry, I had a momentary lapse there.

Mediator: *I asked each of you, in our separate interviews, to think about the things you might want to do or would be willing to do to try to get the job done with the videos, since that seems to be the content issue here.*

George: Well, I think I was pretty clear when I told you what needed to be done.

Mediator: *Yes, and we discovered that that wasn't possible, at least at the first go-around, to get the video time, as I recall. Is that accurate?*

George: Well, I just remembered . . . I told you what was frustrating when I was here before. I'm really getting anxious about this and I clearly know what needs to be done. It's important to me to do my first job in this company very well. I think we probably covered this a number of times.

Angela: We've heard that a lot of times, yes.

Mediator: *One of the things we haven't dealt with is how to get you and Angela cooperating with each other. Is that right?*

George: Well, it seems that, in order to get Angela's cooperation, I am going to have to get on my knees and beg for it.

Mediator: *That isn't what she asked for, if you recall. She didn't ask for you to get on your knees and beg. She asked for some changes in your communication style, but that was difficult for you to hear, though. Correct?*

George: Yes, it is.

Mediator: *So, what about those changes?*

George: She hasn't stopped looking at me. I mean, she's still got the glasses on and she's looking down her nose at me — except now she's looking down her nose toward you.

Mediator: *So, when Angela sits there in her normal way, you see that as her looking down her nose at you. Is that one of the difficulties?*

George: Well, there it is!

Mediator: *That's how you see it, George?*

George: Yes, that's how I see it.

Mediator: *You see, that's not how I see it. I see it as a person with half-glasses on. Angela, do you feel like you're looking down your nose?*

Angela: No.

Mediator: *No. And you've said you're willing to cooperate, haven't you?*

Angela: Yes, I have and I am.

Mediator: *Within certain constraints.*

Angela: Yes.

Mediator: *What are some of those constraints?*

Angela: On my cooperation?

Mediator: *Yes, on your cooperation.*

Angela: Well, I think I told George about how I like to be approached and I don't see him as willing to do that. He keeps jabbing at me. I don't like to be jabbed.

Mediator: *Well, let's take these one at a time. It has been difficult for George to hear the suggestions about his style, hasn't it?*

Angela: I suppose.

Mediator: *What would indicate that it has been difficult for him?*

Angela: Well, he hasn't changed.

Mediator: *Yes, it's been difficult for him. And what is it that George does, in terms of style? You said "jabbing." What do you classify as jabbing?*

Angela: See? There he goes, taking shots at me.

George: I didn't either. She's just trying to control me. She is a control freak. Look at her looking down at me.

Angela: That is not true.

Mediator: *What is not accurate, from your perspective?*

Angela: I don't look down my nose, I just can't see. My eyesight is poor.

Mediator: *It's probably good for George to hear that.*

Angela: And, I am willing to cooperate with a great many people here.

Mediator: *And would you be willing to cooperate with George?*

Angela: Well, we'll see.

Mediator: *George, did you hear that? She's saying that, with certain conditions, she's willing to cooperate with you.*

George: Oh, well, I heard her say it with great reluctance.

Mediator: *Yes, the same kind of reluctance you have when asked to change your communication style — so you're kind of balanced. Those are hard things for all of us to do whenever somebody asks for change. It's difficult both ways.*

Let's talk about generating some options about the video. Let's try to start there and see what can be done.

The issue is not enough video time. Let's do some brainstorming here about ways you could get access to the video lab to get the videos done or maybe use another lab. I don't know. Let's just generate some possibilities; we're not going to decide on solutions here.

What would be some possible things that could be done to unlock this so that, George, you can get your videos done and, Angela, so it wouldn't upset your whole schedule?

Let's just brainstorm. What are some options?

George: I think the video lab guys would work at any hour of the day or night.

Mediator: *Okay, so working some overtime, that's one possibility. What else? Angela, what do you think might possibly be done? You're not committing to this, now. Let's just brainstorm.*

Angela: I don't know if I want to spend time doing this.

Mediator: *Okay. What would you like to deal with first, instead of that?*

Angela: It seems risky to help George.

Mediator: *Okay. In what way?*

Angela: I don't think he'll use what I know and can help him with. I think he will eventually use it against me.

Mediator: *Oh, so one reason it has been hard for you to cooperate is that you feel that George will use that against you, from your perception. In what way might he do that?*

Angela: I think that he'll talk about this process. I think he'll talk about me the way he has already. I think he will go to Harry and talk about what a hero he is without giving me any credit — and I don't know if I'm willing to let him do that.

Mediator: *Could I write these down?*
    You think he'll talk to Harry and say things about you to other people.

Angela: Yes, talk about it.

Mediator: *Okay. And what was the third one you mentioned?*

Angela: I don't think I'll get the credit.

Mediator: *Oh, that he might not share the credit with you.*

Angela: I don't think he'll share the credit. I think he will talk about what a hero he is, with no credit that I have been an important player in this.

Mediator: *So , if that were the scenario, that puts you in a position of you helping George and George getting all the credit.*

Angela: Yes.

Mediator: *If he were willing to make some agreements about this, would that make it easier for you to help him?*

Angela: Yes.

Mediator: *Hmmm. Did you hear that, George?*

George: Yes, I heard that.

Mediator: *What did she say?*

George: She says that she thinks I'm going to tattle to Harry and she says that . . .

Mediator: *Now, she didn't use the word "tattle," did she?*

George: Well that's what she means. Clearly, that's what . . .

Mediator: *What did she say?*

George: She said that I would go to Harry.

Mediator: *Good. Thanks. It's important to get accuracy.*
  Okay, what were . . .

Angela: I'm always scoffed at.

George: See how she is!

Mediator: *One at a time, now.*
  Angela, we gave you attention when you were talking. Now give the same courtesy when George is talking.

George: Then she said that I would go around and say bad things about her to everybody in the organization.

Mediator: *Now, notice that you're focusing on the part that she's upset about and you're forgetting the promise part from her.*
  Did you hear what her promise was? She said if you would not do these certain things, she would be much more willing to cooperate with you and help you.

George: Yes, I guess that's what she said.

Mediator: *Is that what you heard?*

George: I mostly just hear the tone in her voice.

Mediator: *Yes. So even when she says something positive to you and she's holding out an olive branch, you don't see that?*

George: No. It's just annoying me, just the whole point . . .

Angela: (exasperated sigh)

George: See? See what she did?

Angela: It's all about not being believed. I don't know what I have to say to this man.

Mediator: *Just a second, Angela, I'm working on that, okay?*

George, let's just come back to the promise part. It's really important to me that you hear that from her. She's asking that you do some simple things. With you being the professional, is it hard for you to agree on those?

George: Then she's going to help me get my project done?

Mediator: *She says that she's willing to cooperate. I have a feeling that she's got some really creative ideas that will help unlock this thing, and she's not sharing those ideas with you.*

George: The most important thing for me right now (*hitting the table emphatically several times*) is that, Saturday morning when those sales people come in, I have my video, and on Monday, they are ready to go.

Mediator: *That's clear. And what do you think is the key to unlocking that?*

George: Well, Angela says she would.

Mediator: *Well, that's a pretty good hint, isn't it? Do you want to give it a try and see if we could do that?*

George: Sure, I'll do it, if I can get my project done.

Angela: What assurances do I have?

Mediator: *That's what I'm coming back to, Angela, if you could just hang in there for a second, okay? Remember how important it is for you to do things in order and in sequence when you do your job?*

Angela: Yes.

Mediator: *It's the same with me and mediation. If we jump around too fast, then I can't do the work I need to do.*

Angela: I understand that. I mean, order. I like things listed.

Mediator: *Okay.*

So you have three things listed here. Let's take these things one at a time. George, you talked a lot during the interviews about your professionalism and your ability to do things, how you could take on basically any task and get it done. Do these fall into that kind of a category?

George: Talking to Harry falls in that category?

Mediator: *Yes. I mean, agreeing not to talk to Harry and take all the credit.*

George: It would not even occur to me to talk to Harry.

Mediator: *So, that's not hard for you to do at all. So you could agree to it?*

George: He gave me a job to do and I'm on my way. I'm independent. I meet with Harry, but rarely.

Mediator: *Okay. You need to tell Angela that you're not going to talk to Harry separately about this.*

George: Angela, I will not talk to Harry separately.

Angela: Well, I guess since you don't like him much, that's believable.

Mediator: *So we already have one of these items, don't we? He agrees to do that.*

Angela: And if you do, you need to know that I will never help with anything again.

Mediator: *What she is saying is that this is really crucial to her, George. Do you hear how important it is to her?*

George: Yes, I hear that it is important. It's important to me, too, because I think she's got a direct line into Harry. She has a red phone in her office to Harry.

Mediator: *Well, maybe one of the things that will happen, when we get this thing unlocked and get your video produced on time, is that you'll get more access to Harry.*

George: That could be.

Angela: George, if you make Harry look good, then you'll get a red phone.

George: Is that right?

Angela: Yes, you know . . .

George: I want a red phone.

Angela: George will polish his wing tips.

Mediator: *Oh, a pretty good hint. Thanks, Angela. Now, number two — saying things to other people in the organization about Angela.*

George: Saying things to other people in the organization. Now, I have said to you in these interviews that I think that she is a major block, but I don't normally spend a whole lot of time gossiping with people. That's not my style. I've got a project to do and I spend hours on that project. But I don't gossip.

Mediator: *About Angela?*

George: And Angela won't believe this, but I honestly don't have a whole lot of time to talk about her to other people.

Mediator: *Angela, what is your concern here? Have people told you that George is talking about you a lot?*

Angela: I just kind of hear him in the halls.

Mediator: *Does he say your name? That "Angela does this" and "Angela does that"?*

Angela: He kind of mutters. And rolls his eyes. When somebody says, "Angela," George will go . . . (she imitates him).

Mediator: *Oh, so it's not talking about you? It's a non-verbal reaction?*

Angela: Yes.

Mediator: *You know, one of the things that happens in a situation like this is that people show the conflict stress non-verbally. As we get this resolved, that will probably dissipate by itself. If he's not upset at you, he probably won't roll his eyes, that would be my guess.*

Angela: Well, that makes sense.

Mediator: *It often happens, anyway.*

Angela: Is that true?

George: That I'll quit rolling my eyes? I think that if I get cooperation, then I'll have no need to roll my eyes.

Mediator: *Isn't that interesting? You say that if you get cooperation, you won't have to roll your eyes. And she says, if you stop rolling your eyes, I'll cooperate.*

Wow! It looks to me like we've got a basis to work this thing out.

George: Yes, that sounds good.

Mediator: *Okay, so that's number two, and the third one is getting credit with Harry.*

Let's assume for a moment that you get this video produced and that we come up with a way to do this and that you continue to get your work done on time. Can either of you think of a way so that you could both get points with Harry instead of tugging against each other?

Angela: Harry likes no sign of trouble.

Mediator: *Oh, calmness.*

Angela: When he is evaluated by his boss, they kind of hurrah about who can maintain the tightest ship, so that they can play a lot of golf.

Mediator: *So he values . . . ?*

Angela: Smooth operation. So I think if we did this together and made some kind of sign that we had helped maintain that smoothness, that we would both get credit.

George: Well, credit with Harry, I have to tell you, is really high on my list. I mean, I need this project. It's the top of my list.
 And I want Harry to understand that whatever task he gave me, I have done that task, so I need that credit.

Mediator: *I think that's pretty neat that Angela is willing to share with you how to deal with Harry, to say what's important to Harry.*

George: Well, that's helpful. I hadn't thought about it because, frankly, you know, Harry and I haven't had much time together. He brought me in and gave me this project and told me to go.

Mediator: *Well, you're pretty new and haven't had a chance to know him.*

Angela: Well, you know why he doesn't spend much time with people?

George: No.

Angela: Because he doesn't know anything about this business.

George: Harry doesn't know about this business?

Mediator: *We can come back to Harry a little bit later.*

George: Boy, I've got somebody now!

Mediator: *Let's get back to question number three, which is getting credit with Harry. What you're sharing is that, if the two of you do something together around Harry and you don't have to be struggling over this, you can both actually gain more points with him.*

Angela: Yes.

Mediator: *If we get it so calm, so there aren't any waves going on, that sort of thing. . . .*
 George, what would you like to see happen here?

George: I'd like to make sure that he understands that I have put in an enormous amount of effort and time getting this project, which is normally a four-month project, down to less than two months.

Mediator: *My impression is that he already knows that. The issue for him is the struggle between the two of you.*

George: That's the only thing he understands right now?

Mediator: *Yes. He's blocked by that. It bugs the hell out of him and he's paying me to come in.*

George: Okay.

Mediator: *George, are you willing to make an offer to Angela?*

Angela: By the way, the reason why he invited you in was because Sam, his colleague, invited a mediator in — and he's competitive.

Mediator: *Well, whatever works, right?*

Angela: Yes.

Mediator: *My concern is not his motivation. My concern is that the two of you are able to turn around your working relationship so that you don't hate each other for the rest of your lives — or the rest of your tenure in this organization.*

Angela: I guess I said that because I wanted George to hear that, how Harry . . .

Mediator: *I see. You're trying to tell George how Harry thinks and operates.*
Okay, how about if the two of you are able to work this out, then you go to Harry together and say, "We worked through an issue that we thought was impossible and we got both videos done and we feel really good about it," or whatever the appropriate thing might be. Would that be possible?

Angela: I would be willing to do that.

George: Sounds good to me. I need the success.

Angela: I do want to tell you how to act around him. He has a very strict code of how one approaches him and I know you don't like that — but it really is important.

Mediator: *Angela, let's put that down as an agenda item. After we solve the video thing, we'll come back and talk about dealing with Harry, because I think those are probably good insights. We'll come back to that.*

Angela: Okay.

Mediator: *Where we started was that you were saying there were things that you needed from George before you could come up with some creative solutions for solving this. Do you feel like those have been met?*

Angela: Yes, I do.

Mediator: *Terrific! Good for you! So now let's talk about scheduling the videotape, okay?*

George: When are we going to talk about her looking down her nose at me?

Mediator: *Well, we could talk about that first, or do the video time question first, whatever.*

George: Well, I just noticed that those were her three points and I agree with those three points. But I'm feeling like I don't have three points up there.

Mediator: *Well, you have a big point up there — which is scheduling the video. How about if we do the scheduling of the video time, and then come back to her communication style and some things about your communication style?*

George: The video time is most important.

Mediator: *Yes, you said that to me earlier.*
  Is that all right with you, Angela?

Angela: Yes.

Mediator: *Okay. Let's talk about the video time. What are some options?*

Angela: The key is John.

Mediator: *How is he the key?*

Angela: He is the one who has the informal influence at the video shop and he's the one who throws the parties to get people to stay up all night. They're all big partyers.

Mediator: *So we're talking about strategies with the video lab and John is the key to this?*

Angela: Yes. They get sort of a kick out of doing "Can we pull this off?"

Mediator: *Like the challenge?*

Angela: Like a challenge. But they have to know that you're going to support them. I mean, there are some things they want for their lab and they've got to know that George will be there for them.

Mediator: *So, if they feel like George will be in their corner and help them out — maybe in getting new equipment or whatever is important to them — they'd really go that extra mile?*

Angela: I think so. And since this is for an important product line, that may be the leverage to get that equipment.

Mediator: *Good idea.*

George: I don't see a problem with that, because I think that those guys really like me. I'd probably be at the party.

Angela: Yes, you would. Now, don't tell anybody that I talked about the parties, okay?

Mediator: *Could you agree to that, George? It's obviously important to her.*

George: Absolutely.

Mediator: *So, one strategy is to get overtime from the lab people. That's what we're talking about here. What would be some other things that could be done?*

George: I'm willing to work all night long on this project, so I don't have to do this in the daytime. I work really well at night.

Angela: And I don't.

Mediator: *Right. You work better from eight to five.*

Angela: I only work from eight to five.

Mediator: *Right. So if you worked eight to five, and if the two of you could convince John and his folks that you would support them, and they could give you the video time — if you're accurate on that Angela, would that give you enough time to get your video done, George?*

George: If I used the next three evenings, I'd be able to do it.

Mediator: *Great.*

George: I wouldn't even have to work all night, although I'd be willing to do that.

Mediator: *Okay, that's one really good option. Now, is there anything about that option that would not work that the two of you can see?*
This is presuming we could get them to agree, which would probably involve the two of you going to them together — which, by the way, could be fun. To see the two of you going together to see them would kind of blow their minds.

Angela: They'd be tickled by that.

Mediator: *They'd love it. It would probably make the party.*

Angela: It would be good gossip material.

Mediator: *Let's see, George and Angela walk in together . . .*

Angela: And I don't have my glasses.

As the discussion continued, the mediator helped George and Angela fine-tune their agreements and make additional ones to avoid trouble with one another in the future.

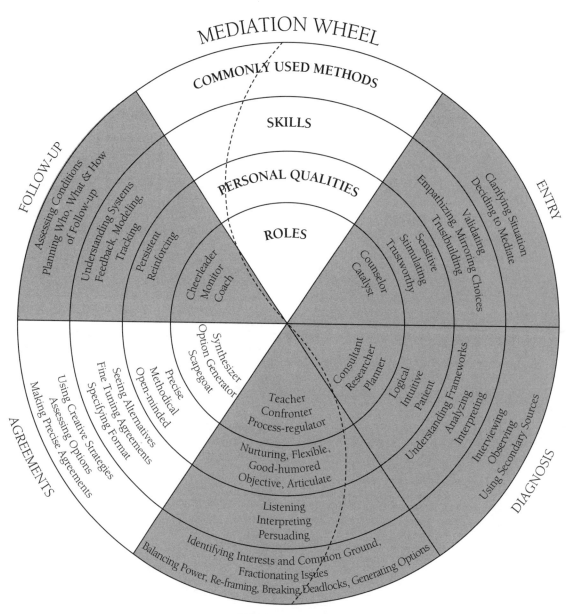

MEDIATION WHEEL

COMMONLY USED METHODS

SKILLS

PERSONAL QUALITIES

ROLES

ENTRY

Clarifying Situation
Deciding to Mediate

Validating
Empathizing, Mirroring Choices
Trustbuilding

Sensitive
Stimulating
Trustworthy

Counselor
Catalyst

DIAGNOSIS

Understanding Frameworks
Analyzing
Interpreting

Interviewing
Observing
Using Secondary Sources

Logical
Intuitive
Patient

Consultant
Researcher
Planner

Teacher
Confronter
Process-regulator

Nurturing, Flexible,
Good-humored
Objective, Articulate

Listening
Interpreting
Persuading

NEGOTIATION

Identifying Interests and Common Ground,
Fractionating Issues
Balancing Power, Re-framing, Breaking Deadlocks, Generating Options

AGREEMENTS

Using Creative Strategies
Assessing Options
Making Precise Agreements

Seeing Alternatives
Fine Tuning Agreements
Specifying Format

Precise
Methodical
Open-minded

Synthesizer
Option Generator
Scapegoat

Cheerleader
Monitor
Coach

Persistent
Reinforcing

Understanding Systems
Feedback, Modeling,
Tracking

Assessing Conditions
Planning Who, What & How
of Follow-up

FOLLOW-UP

MEDIATION STAGE IV: AGREEMENTS

M EDIATION SKILLS PRODUCE AGREEMENTS THAT COVER THE KEY ISSUES of the conflict — and leave the disputants feeling settled, not rushed or resentful. Appealing though it may be to speed to agreements, resist the temptation to "strike while the iron is hot." Experience shows that hurried agreements only create situations that may spawn further conflict.

To make durable agreements that serve the interests of all parties, the mediator needs to:

- ▶ Agree on the agreements.

- ▶ Know and use creative agreement strategies.

- ▶ Decide on the form of agreement.

- ▶ Do a sabotage assessment.

- ▶ End the mediation constructively.

Here, you are in a more directive stage of the mediation process, helping participants move toward closure, making sure that all parties are feeling settled, finished and treated fairly while pushing for specificity in the agreement to sustain the goodwill generated during the mediation. Consult the Mediation Wheel for alignment during this stage.

Agreeing on Agreements

Before addressing the details of the final agreement, the mediator and conflict participants often need to make a pre-agreement of sorts — rather like a prenuptial agreement — to answer any or all of the following questions:

When is an agreement an agreement?

Representatives of a federal agency thought that when they had responded to the concerns of the city council about a local land use issue, an agreement was reached. Each time the agency responded, however, the council added new concerns, so that the process dragged on for two years. Not having an agreement on what constituted an agreement led to animosity and a hardening of positions that prevented moving toward a decision. Consequently, when mediation began, the first agreement had to be what document, in what form, presented at what time, ratified by what method and by whom, would constitute an agreement. The resulting agreement on the agreement was that:

1. The parties at the bargaining table were empowered to make an agreement, taking previously discussed concerns into account.

2. The document they produced was to be reviewed for legal implications.

3. The City Council would then vote yes or no on the document, rather than vote on raising additional concerns.

4. After the City Council vote, the final document would be put into a legal form signed by all parties.

This detailed pre-agreement highlights several questions to be answered to prevent a growing — and sometimes explosive — sense of betrayal. Remember that when people in conflict have begun to lower their guards, speak more honestly about their real concerns and even enjoy the give-and-take of more constructive conflict, it is of particular importance to remember that the mediation process is not yet complete.

What will constitute a final agreement?

Sometimes it is important to specify what form the final agreement will take before you reach the last stages of mediation. If one party wants a legally binding agreement and another wants a handshake, the form of the agreement itself can trigger issues of trust. Legality may signal trust to one party while it symbolizes mistrust to the other, who regards a handshake as the only proper way to seal an agreement between equals. A clarification up front may bypass this potential stumbling block. Or the mediator may need to re-frame the issue by asking, "Will the specifics and language of a legal document undermine any of the gains you have made in the conflict?" Or, "Can there be some other way to symbolize trust between you two, other than the form of the agreement?"

What is the process of the final ratification?

As the example of the city council illustrated, a pre-agreement should specify if the people at the table have the final say or whether others must sign off on the agreement. A pre-agreement should also indicate a process for refinement, if other people signing off have reservations, and specify how many times the reviews and refinements may occur.

Creative Agreement Strategies

Many times after diagnosing and discussing conflict issues, you may find that differences are not really in conflict or that solutions are readily apparent. Other times, issues are tougher to resolve and developing solid agreements may require tapping into a variety of agreement strategies. These strategies to prompt collaboration are in no particular order, but are offered as a tool kit to be used when appropriate.

Expanding the pie or sweetening the pot involves increasing the perception of resources being considered in the negotiation. It involves asking what other things, people or events the person values so you can trade on those. One party may not be able to give on a central issue but may provide the other party with something even more valued. One of us was asked to work for far less than our normal fee and, if money had been the only consideration, agreement would have been impossible. But the work was in New Orleans — a place of considerable appeal — which added to the pie.

Creative compensation can be content (as in money), process (as in greater autonomy) or relationship (an apology). The mediator can help the parties reach agreement by having one reward the other for conceding with some other form of compensation. One party may get agreement from the executive committee on the type of decision making to be used, while the other party is given greater autonomy in his/her department. Sometimes people want to be compensated for past "wrongs" in order to reach agreements. Other times a person may simply want an apology. The mediator may ask directly, "What would compensate you for your loss and allow you to reach agreement?"

One way to make certain that one party does not leave the sessions feeling martyred or resentful is to ask directly. "You have given up things that are important to you. How might you feel compensated for those concessions?" If important feelings are disregarded, they may arise later to sabotage the agreement or create another conflict.

Cost cutting involves finding a way to minimize the emotional cost to one party for going along with the other party. A new procedure may be adopted to accommodate one party but delaying its implementation may make it less detrimental to the other, for instance. One manager may give a colleague access to the labs but want him to phone before coming to use them, in order to minimize disrupting the work. Some companies ask that the financial agreements of lawsuits not be publicized, for example. The mediator can ask, "Is there anything that we can do to take the sting out of the agreement for you?"

Logrolling is a variation that involves one party agreeing on issues of highest priority and conceding on another issue of lesser importance. In one situation described in *The Mediation Process*, an employer would not pay a consultant for unsatisfactory work. The consultant wanted the money, but was more interested in the principle of having the debt paid. They agreed that the employer would pay the consultant's fee to a charity of the employer's choice. This agreement met the primary principle of each party.[1]

Bridging occurs when a totally new option is developed that satisfies all the people involved. For example, one department head agreed that a new information system was needed, but would not complete the work necessary to begin operating it. The manager responsible for implementing the system was baffled by the resistance until he explored some underlying interests and realized that recognition and creativity were essential to the resistant department head. They devised an agreement whereby the resistant party could modify the system to meet his needs and would take credit for those modifications when presenting the program to the executive team. New options can be created when there is a thorough understanding of all interests involved.

Alternating is another possible solution that involves having parties alternate between the options each favors. For example, in one quarter the team operates one way, in another, the second way.

Compromise literally means splitting the difference and involves somehow dividing the available resources. Compromise is useful for establishing goodwill, resolving a conflict that seems difficult to do in other ways or providing an intermediate strategy that lays the groundwork for future negotiations. Compromise should be considered almost as a last resort, however, since it rarely satisfies the key interests of the parties. Unions and management may split the difference in settling a dispute over compensation issues, but the compromise does not address the employees' underlying needs both to be valued and to have greater influence in decision making. These unmet needs form the basis for the next round of conflicts.

Making agreements of varying strengths can sometimes produce movement when the negotiation is stuck. The mediator may suggest that, instead of instituting a policy permanently, the parties use it only temporarily, as an experiment, in order to test its effectiveness. Then, perhaps six months later, the policy may be changed or refined.

Stronger Agreements Are:	*Weaker Agreements Are:*
Substantive. They define specific tangible exchanges (money, services, labor, etc.) that will result from negotiations.	*Procedural.* They merely define the process by which a decision is to be made.
Comprehensive. They include a resolution of all issues in dispute.	*Partial.* They do not include a resolution of all issues in dispute.
Permanent. They resolve for all time issues in dispute.	*Provisional.* They make temporary trial decisions that may be subject to change in the future.
Final. They include all the details in their final form.	*In-principle.* They include general agreements, but details remain to be worked out.
Non-conditional. They end the dispute without requiring future conditional performance.	*Contingent.* They state that the conclusion of the dispute is conditional upon additional information or performance by one or more parties.
Binding. People agree to be bound and to adhere to the terms of settlement, often to the extent of identifying consequences if a party does not follow through.	*Non-binding.* The agreement is a recommendation or request to which none of the parties guarantees adherence.[2]

Forms of Agreement

Often, a "release of stress" comes at the agreement stage, and novice mediators may then read this as a sign to stop the process. After all, if you and the disputing parties are feeling relieved, doesn't that solve the problem? Unfortunately, it doesn't.

Without a firm, spelled-out agreement, all the work up to this point can simply evaporate. Making decisions about the forms and details of agreements is crucial. Feeling better is not the criterion for success. The end product of a successful, effective mediation is a workable, follow-able, useful agreement.

Agreements can be oral or take some written form, from a Memorandum of Agreement to a legally binding document. Each has strengths and weaknesses. **Oral agreements** are easy to reach. The mediator in talking with the disputants has found ways to help them manage their dispute. The weakness of oral agreements should be obvious. As Sam Goldwin said, "Verbal contracts aren't worth the paper they're printed on."

The spoken word is likely to become the basis for further misunderstanding and discord, especially between people who have been in conflict and undoubtedly have a history of misunderstanding one another's intentions and actions. It may be against the culture of the company to put things in writing, however, forcing you to conclude with an oral agreement. In such instances, take a few precautions.

1. Review the agreement carefully, step by step.

2. Ask the participants for their interpretation of it: "Sharon, what is your understanding of the two major parts of this agreement?"

3. Urge the participants to take notes as you review the agreement. Generally, it is unwise simply to heave a sigh of relief and be glad it's all over. Remember, you were brought into the dispute because the participants were out of control with one another, and those patterns of interaction can easily re-emerge.

4. Finally, with an oral agreement, it's wise to set a "check-in" time later on, when all those involved will meet with you to review their progress in keeping their agreements.

The most common form of agreement in an organizational context is a **Memorandum of Agreement**, a written statement reviewed and signed by the parties who then receive identical copies. It is similar to the single text negotiation strategy described on page 142, where participants continue to review the written agreement until they agree on each point of the document.

A Memorandum of Agreement needs to be complete, specific and include time frames clearly spelled out. The only items left out of a memorandum are those that are sensitive to the organization or those that would cause a dispute with someone not in the original negotiation. There may be privileged technical information that should only be seen inside the company, for example. Or, two employees may agree on how they will "handle" their boss, an agreement that may be misunderstood by that boss who will see the agreement.

No item or process is too small or too inconsequential to include in an agreement. One dispute was resolved this way:

John: I agree to clean my desk each Monday morning, beginning next Monday.

Peggy: I will say hello to my fellow workers each day and not walk away from them without talking, starting tomorrow.

Lance: I will meet with each employee and go over my evaluations of their performance three times a year before I do the written annual evaluation in March. I'll meet them outside the office for a minimum of one hour for each person. The first round of informal evaluation and feedback sessions will begin April 30.

Pat: I will no longer take lunch at my desk. I'll have lunch with someone in the office at least two days a week, starting tomorrow.

In another dispute among three medical partners, the memorandum looked slightly different. Here is Round One of assessing the issues, Round Two of framing them into interests, the first Memorandum of Agreement and the Addendum. We hope these convey a sense of how the mediation unfolded.

Medical Associates Partnership: Marvin, Sam and Barry
Round One
Issues

Marvin

- Communication — can't talk with Sam and Barry.
- Monday meetings are "nitpicky." Energy needs to be constructive.
- I want Sam to smile and be nice to me.
- I want Barry to smile and be more relaxed.
- Sam's relationship with the staff outside the office. He is not kind to them.
- Sam thinks he is being cheated financially.
- I want even moods (Sam is unpredictable).
- I need more feedback from the others.
- I want to be corrected, but don't want them to be condescending to me.

Sam

- I want Marvin to work better in the context of the organization.
- Decisions are too independent. I want them made as a team.
- Marvin's problems with sexual harassment need to be left behind us. They have been addressed. I want to move on.
- Marvin "unloads" on patients and gets too emotionally involved. There is tension in the office as a result of this.
- We need better communication with the patients; the quality of "patient care" is an issue.
- Marvin and Barry appear to carry grudges about the original contract I signed when joining. I just want to keep things equal.
- Quality of care is an issue (specifically with Marvin).
- We need to have better patient charts. Information is not entered on the charts.
- Productivity and quality of care are issues.

Barry

- Marvin's insincerity with the patients — he "lays it on too thick." Steve, the practice administrator, thinks so too.
- Disagreements with other professionals in town are embarrassing. Marvin gets into arguments with architects and builders.
- Marvin is unpredictable. Thirteen years ago he went to Florida looking for a job, which makes me wonder about his commitment here.

- Marvin promises to stop his touching behavior, but doesn't.
- Sam's behavior in the office — he is uptight, hard to talk to, aloof and dumps on Marvin.
- More contentment between partners.
- Partners should take more time off.
- Marvin's "frantic" behavior and excessive volume.

Medical Associates
Round Two
Grouping of Issues

Between Marvin and Sam

- Expectations for patient care.
- When and how to signal the need for help on procedures.
- Complete information on lab tests, chart, and talks with patients and families.
- Interphysician communication.
- How to find out what is on your mind — both positively and negatively.
- Spending time together at a regular time or away from the office routine.

Between Sam and Barry

- Sam turns to him for decisions and Barry feels burdened.

Between Barry and Marvin

- Marvin's touching behavior.

Team Issues

- Information about patients and concerns about them.
- Use of "we" and "our" language rather than "I/my."
- Continue Monday sessions as a team. Will have two sessions, with Steve not present at the second session.
- Complaints in the office go to Steve. Steve will talk to the staff and supervise them.
- Quality of care. Need speed on information. Will not criticize the third doctor to the other one.
- Rules for referring patients:
    when want a second opinion
    when cannot handle the problem
    if the patient desires/requires it

Medical Associates
Memorandum of Agreement

▸ Sam will continue to use the services of an accountant separate from the corporate accountant.

▸ Sam will be given time to check decisions of the partnership team before final agreements are reached.

▸ Marvin will secure the services of a personal attorney. His present attorney will finish work in progress but all new work will go to the new attorney.

▸ On information flow:

　▸ Staff complaints will be referred to Steve, the practice administrator.

　▸ If one partner has concerns about another, he will contact that person directly and will neither complain to the third partner nor use the third partner as a go-between.

　▸ If a partner is approached by another concerning the third the partner will encourage the concerned partner to talk directly with the third person.

　▸ When a partner desires information about the operation of the practice, he will secure the information from Steve and not from other staff members.

▸ To facilitate quality care, patient information will be complete. This includes charts, lab tests and communication with the patient and family. All this information will be shared with any partner who gets involved with the patient.

▸ To facilitate a team operation, the partners will refer to "our" practice and use "we" rather than "my practice" and "I."

▸ Barry and Sam will not take any unilateral action regarding possible sexual harassment. Marvin will continue seeing his psychiatrist.

▸ We agree to the above understandings and will follow these principles in order to have a smoothly functioning partnership.

These agreements were entered into in good faith.

(Signed)

Marvin _____ Date _____

Sam _____ Date _____

Barry _____ Date _____

Medical Associates
Addendum to Agreement

The three partners will tell Steve:

- ► to prepare a common agenda for the management meetings.
- ► that the partners will have a separate meeting following the management meeting in order to communicate directly with one another on issues that can best be discussed in private.
- ► that all employee complaints except those dealing with quality of medical care will be referred to Steve.

In the event that a staff member approaches a partner regarding a quality of care issue:

- ► There will be no reprimand of the employee. He or she will be complimented for having the best interests of Eye Associates as a goal.
- ► The care issue will be discussed directly with the other partner.
- ► The resolution of the issue will be communicated back to the staff member.

These agreements are an addendum, mutually agreed to on March 13, 1991.

(Signed)

Marvin _____ Date _____

Sam _____ Date _____

Barry _____ Date _____

Process Suggestions for Partnership Meetings:

- ► Focus on interests, not positions. Always ask yourself, "What is my main interest? What do I want, in general terms?"
- ► Separate the people from the problem. Focus on the problem to be solved, not the individual involved.
- ► Generate multiple solutions. Always suggest at least three ways to solve a problem or meet a goal.

Notice this agreement is specific and clear. And, it came in two stages. These partners met with the mediator at a resort for a weekend and, by the end of Saturday night, had reached agreement. Sunday, they went over the agreement in detail. The conflicts between the partners erupted again, so the agreement was amended. Finally, they agreed to all additional aspects of the agreement and were able to carry out the agreement for the next two years.

Agreements also can be in the form of **legally binding documents**. This, of course, adds an enforcement mechanism to an agreement which can become important if an agreement involves large sums of money, other tangible resources and/or contracts. It is important, however, that the legal process not drive the agreement. The legal process should (1) accurately reflect what both parties want and (2) should not be allowed to create a further dispute. Often the process of working with attorneys tends to drive the parties apart, with each seeking maximum advantage. The attorneys should be working for agreement, not driving new wedges of discord and misunderstanding between the parties.

Mediating when a legal document is necessary, we follow these steps:

1. The memorandum of agreement is carefully reviewed and distributed to the parties.

2. Agreement is reached about which attorneys will be involved and the process to be followed: Ted will ask Sarah, attorney for the firm, to do the first draft, for example.

3. Both parties review the agreement with the mediator before signing off on it.

The most common error in situations demanding legally binding documents is to turn the process over to the attorneys, who often inadvertently create further discord. Remember, the legal system is designed to be adversarial while mediation focuses on finding agreement and common ground between the disputing parties. Combining

the legal expertise of attorneys with the process expertise and consensus building skills of mediators builds wise agreements that also
have the force of law.

Regardless of the form, an agreement needs to be specific.
Consider the following:

Agreement Details

▸ Criteria for compliance: How will we know we have succeeded?
  These are do-able, measurable actions that indicate success.

▸ General and specific steps to implement the agreement.

▸ Time lines for implementing each action.

▸ Person primarily accountable for each action and people with
  secondary and supporting roles.

▸ Procedural agreements to prevent future conflicts.

▸ Procedures to manage perceived or actual violations of the
  settlement.

The last two items are extremely important to the overall durability of an agreement. The mediator may ask, "Now that this dispute is
managed successfully, what would each of you need to do to keep
disputes like this from arising again?"

Procedures to manage perceived violations could include agreements to:

▸ Check with each other before escalating the conflict.

▸ Involve the same or another agreed-upon mediator before the
  conflict increases.

▸ Use a mutually agreed-upon grievance procedure to regulate the
  conflict, and/or

▸ Use another form of conflict resolution if this agreement does not
  stick.

Disputants might agree to further mediation with the same mediator or a new one, arbitration or a specific, defined court process.

Following one agreement, Tom and Bruce agreed to talk directly with one another if they had concerns about the other and not to talk to other people before checking with each other. Further, they agreed to meet on a specific date to assess how they were doing at following their agreement.

In another conflict, participants said, "We agree that in the case of further dispute both will meet with the mediator and not file any legal action until we meet with the mediator."

Sabotage Check

As with the Medical Associates, those in conflict often need time to think about the agreement before it is put in final form. During the interim, conducting what we call a "sabotage check" gives participants a chance to legitimately voice both their reservations and their knowledge about how the agreement could fail. The mediator can ask what reservations or concerns each party has about the agreement: "What have you been holding back? Are there gnawing, uneasy feelings you have about any part of this agreement?" Or even more directly, "Now, tell me, what are all the ways we can screw up this agreement? Let's brainstorm ways that either those of us here at the table or other forces in the organization can block effective implementation." Issues that arise should be listed and ways to reduce the resistance incorporated into the agreement.

A "Sabotage Check" serves a number of purposes. It allows disputants to reveal the "dirty tricks" lingering just below the surface and often provides a source of humor and tension release. Most interestingly, it seems to "inoculate" the parties against actually doing the sabotage. We find it a very effective way of preventing sabotage from arising later.

Members of one department in a hospital had agreed to confront each other directly when they perceived a problem, rather than going to others to gossip and gain support for their point of view. They all knew they had to change this conflict-producing pattern both to increase efficiency and decrease their stress. But, when asked what might prevent them from using their new norm, they easily listed more than half a dozen things, including habit, fear of what the other would do when confronted and losing their method of building closeness — because they felt close to those with whom they gossiped. So, the agreement was expanded to include training in conflict management, role-playing confrontations in staff meetings and holding social events to reduce the power of the barriers of habit, fear and loss of closeness.

A useful technique here is the force field analysis. Have disputants list all the forces (personal desire and motivation, interpersonal motivations, skills and organizational forces like leadership or structure) that support the agreement and all the forces that hinder it. The goal is to increase the driving or supportive forces and decrease the hindering or restraining forces — which includes identifying the opportunities for sabotage.

Force Field Analysis

Goal: Conflict directly rather than build coalitions through gossip.

Driving Force		Restraining Force
Desire to reduce stress	←→	Habit
Efficiency	←→	Fear of failure
Key leaders pushing the change	←→	Loss of closeness
Disastrous results in past	←→	Lack of conflict skills

Action steps to increase driving forces and reduce restraining ones:
1. Conflict training
2. Role playing
3. New ways to get close

Ending the Mediation

An appropriate ending for a mediation can increase the parties' commitment to their agreement and set the stage for follow-up work that solidifies workable and durable agreements. Here are a few ideas to end the mediation and tie up any loose ends into a pleasant package.

Review the process used

This helps people understand the mediation and allows them to use parts of the process in any future disputes. Remember, one of the goals of mediation is to teach people to manage conflicts more constructively. A review can also provide feedback to the mediator on his/her strengths and weaknesses. Reviewing also provides one more opportunity to check for any residual resentments that might be lurking below the surface.

Have participants articulate promises included in the agreement

These could be statements in staff or company meetings of their intent to correct certain problems, or press or information releases to other media, or statements for staff or in-house newsletters. Public promises tend to increase commitment — like telling friends you intend to stop smoking.

Have a symbolic exchange of gifts or tokens of affection or cooperation

In western culture, we often overlook the healing and sealing importance of ritual gift-giving. Native Americans have used both sharing a peace pipe and the ritual exchange of gifts to symbolize their good faith. We have to create our own symbols, but they needn't be overly serious. One work team, to commemorate having made important decisions toward dramatic new directions and having begun to heal many old wounds, gave out new mugs that said, "The Status Quo Ain't No Mo."

Create symbolic events to signal the end of the mediation

An event can celebrate goodwill and the hard work of reaching agreements, and perhaps demonstrate new or renewed friendship.

The event can be as simple as a handshake, as celebratory as a banquet or as formal as a ceremonial presentation of signed agreements to those in authority.

In this stage of mediation, you are scouting for any invisible piano wires on which participants may hang themselves, helping them to be precise and detailed about ways in which they can solve their conflicts and prevent future ones. Then you may well celebrate success.

APPLICATION

▸ The **Checklist for Agreements** provides an overall guide for reaching satisfactory, workable agreements.

YARBROUGH
GROUP

Checklist for Agreements
Have you:

☐ Made preliminary agreements on the agreement, if necessary?

☐ Considered the alternatives for reaching creative agreements that leave the least resentment or feelings of loss?

☐ Included even "small" things, like changes in interpersonal behavior?

☐ Clarified the form the agreement needs to take — oral, written or legal?

☐ Attended to the interpersonal feelings to know if the agreement is really solid?

☐ Given people time to test out the agreement — or at least think about it overnight?

☐ Been highly specific in the agreement, to reduce ambiguity and the possibility of future resentment?

☐ Done a sabotage check of how the parties could interfere with the agreement and then altered the agreement accordingly?

☐ Discussed how to prevent similar disputes from arising again?

☐ Indicated the process to use if there is a perceived violation?

☐ Paid attention to ending the agreement with a review of the process?

☐ Found an appropriate way to symbolize closure and agreement?

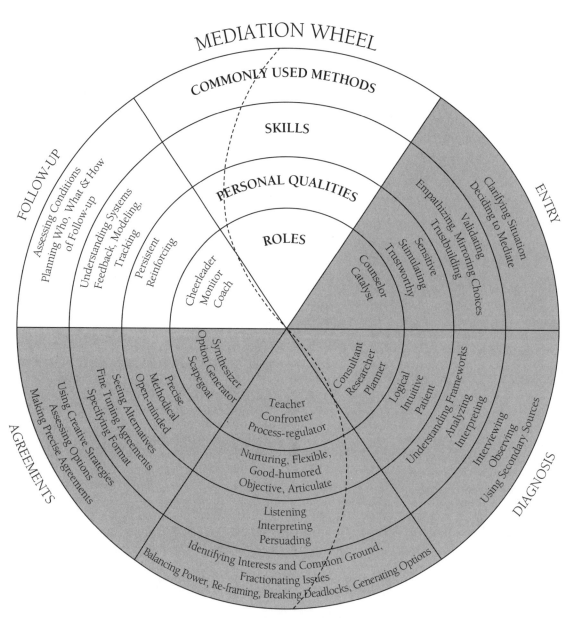

MEDIATION WHEEL

COMMONLY USED METHODS

SKILLS

PERSONAL QUALITIES

ROLES

FOLLOW-UP

ENTRY

DIAGNOSIS

NEGOTIATION

AGREEMENTS

Assessing Conditions
Planning Who, What & How
of Follow-up

Understanding Systems
Feedback, Modeling,
Tracking

Persistent
Reinforcing

Cheerleader
Monitor
Coach

Clarifying Situation
Deciding to Mediate

Validating
Empathizing, Mirroring Choices
Trustbuilding

Sensitive
Stimulating
Trustworthy

Counselor
Catalyst

Consultant
Researcher
Planner

Logical
Intuitive
Patient

Understanding Frameworks
Analyzing
Interpreting

Interviewing
Observing
Using Secondary Sources

Synthesizer
Option Generator
Scapegoat

Precise
Methodical
Open-minded

Using Creative Strategies
Assessing Options
Making Precise Agreements

Seeing Alternatives
Fine Tuning Agreements
Specifying Format

Teacher
Confronter
Process-regulator

Nurturing, Flexible,
Good-humored
Objective, Articulate

Listening
Interpreting
Persuading

Identifying Interests and Common Ground,
Fractionating Issues
Balancing Power, Re-framing, Breaking Deadlocks, Generating Options

MEDIATION STAGE V: FOLLOW-UP

ONE OF THE MOST COMMON MISTAKES IN MEDIATING ORGANIZATIONAL disputes is to assume that, once agreements have been reached, then it's back to business as usual. Even the best, clearest and most specific agreements need monitoring, so follow-up is a vital last step in the mediation process. Changing habitual behavior is hard in any situation, and even more difficult when those behaviors have been embedded in the context of an organization that may, in fact, have supported dysfunctional, conflict-producing patterns.

Following up mediation supports the disputants who will need reinforcement, helps insure that agreements will endure and demonstrates that management is serious about supporting constructive conflict. Reviewing the conditions of the agreement can reveal the intensity of the follow-up required.

Assessment Conditions

▸ Trust between the parties.

▸ Simplicity of the agreement.

▸ Skill level of the people who will implement the agreement.

▸ Congruence between organizational culture and the agreement.

▸ Investment in the agreement.

▸ Power equity between the parties.

In general, the lower the degree of any of these conditions, the greater the need to scrutinize the agreement and support its implementation. For example, if agreement has been reached but the parties still have a fundamental mistrust of each other, the monitoring plan should be more stringent. This might include more frequent meetings to check on progress, developing ways to rebuild the trust, maybe even restructuring work so old animosities don't resurface. Similarly, if the organizational culture does not support the sort of new communication patterns the agreement calls for, rest assured that all kinds of forces will be at work to undermine the agreement. Disputants may need to construct parallel organizational structures to insure communication, like meetings other than the regular staff meetings, where communication generally is directed toward the boss and not one another.

Follow-Up Guidelines

A follow-up plan needs to specify *how, who* and *what*.

How will the agreement be monitored?

Disputants need to agree on the times and means for checking their agreements and monitoring their progress. Weekly staff meetings, private meetings, feedback solicited from others affected by the conflict, follow-up meetings with the mediator or other in-house resources could all provide ways of affirming successes and supporting needed changes. Specific times need to be set, usually with more frequent check-ins in the beginning, tapering off as the changes become more routine.

Who will monitor?

Whether internal or external to the organization, the mediator needs to provide guidance in the follow-up. If the mediation has gone well, disputants often grow to trust the mediator and feel supported when he/she encourages and coaches them as they implement their agreement.

Others outside the mediation process should also be considered — and, at this stage, may prove even more useful. For example, in-house Human Resources people can be available to answer questions, to coach disputants or to support them privately and publicly. A manager who has the ear of top leaders could meet with disputants, provide feedback on improvements and also champion organizational changes to further support constructive conflict management. Disputants could also agree to use a committee of supportive subordinates, co-workers and/or superiors with a stake in the outcome, to provide guidance and to review progress implementing the agreement.

Regardless of who is selected to help with follow-up, it is critical to specify their role. Will they review and assess? Enforce or oversee? Or perhaps be a cheerleader for the parties? Will they assist parties in modifying agreements if necessary? Will they provide information on the progress of the agreement to other stakeholders? Their role has to be clearly agreed to by the parties, otherwise the goals of the follow-up will be undermined and new conflict likely will erupt.

What will be monitored?

Remember, at this tender stage of the process, the fragile, new behaviors trying to emerge need nurturing, caring and guidance. This means *it is not appropriate* for monitors to find fault and try to catch people making mistakes. Rather, their role is to support them, to help fine-tune their agreements in order to make them more effective, to help devise mid-course corrections and to celebrate their success. As in the mediation, monitoring the workability of the agreement means trying to make the agreement workable, not trying to blame or pinpoint someone supposedly causing problems.

Follow-ups can also focus on changes in organizational structure or procedures to bolster agreements. This might mean implementing changes in the evaluation process or altering the reward structure to support collaboration, for instance.

Helping participants to use the procedures they agreed on in the event of a perceived violation helps make sure the conflict does not escalate again.

Finally, monitors can assist disputants in getting additional support for implementing their agreements. This could include training in conflict or other skills, coaching from others inside or outside the organization, counseling, therapy or consultation on how to restructure the department or organization to prevent similar disputes.

Returning to the Mediation Wheel, notice that the Follow-up Stage moves back toward a balance of directive and receptive skills. This means being persistent in helping people close the process and, at the same time, supporting and encouraging them in making changes that may well be difficult.

APPLICATION

▸ The **Overall Mediation Checklist** provides a reminder of all the significant steps of the process from entry through agreements.

YARBROUGH
GROUP

Overall Mediation Checklist

Stage I: Entry

Have you:

☐ Clarified how the process began so that all parties are on board and empowered?

☐ Explained your role and established credibility?

☐ Explained the steps of mediation?

☐ Indicated precisely what *you* need and what will be expected of the parties?

☐ Explored the consequences of not proceeding?

Stage II: Diagnosis

Have you:

☐ Gathered enough data via interviews and observations to know the issues?

☐ Looked at all process elements of conflict to know key issues?

☐ Considered organizational pressures on the conflict?

☐ Informed the stakeholders about possible ramifications to the dispute — such as changes to be considered if these agreements are to be durable and future conflicts are to be avoided?

☐ Precisely completed a diagnostic planning sheet to organize the conflict process?

Stage III: Negotiation
Have you:

☐ Introduced the mediation thoroughly?

☐ Established common ground?

☐ Let parties vent if necessary?

☐ Established an agenda acceptable to all parties?

☐ Broken conflict into manageable parts?

☐ Framed the conflict in such a way that all understand what they can gain by cooperating and what they can lose by competing?

☐ Balanced power between parties so that one does not dominate the other?

☐ Made it clear that there are unpleasant consequences if they are stuck and refuse to move?

☐ Generated different ways of meeting interests?

☐ Assessed the options using agreed-upon criteria?

Stage IV: Agreements

Have you:

☐ Agreed on when an agreement is an agreement?

☐ Used creative strategies to reach a solid agreement?

☐ Done a sabotage check to find why the agreement will not work and then adjusted the agreement?

☐ Checked the agreement more than once?

☐ Specified *who* will do *what, when?*

☐ Reached agreement on the *form* of the agreement — oral, written, legal?

☐ Taken organizational elements — culture, leadership, procedures, structure — into account to check whether the agreement will stick?

☐ Reviewed the *process*, having participants notice what went well?

☐ Reached agreement on how to prevent future similar conflicts?

☐ Made plans to notify stakeholders of the outcome?

☐ Found an appropriate way to celebrate the agreement and to symbolize goodwill?

Stage V: Follow-up
Have you:

☐ Assessed the conditions that influence the intensity of the follow-up?

☐ Decided who will monitor the agreement?

☐ Decided on what will be monitored for how long?

☐ Made any long-range organizational plans for improving the conditions that contribute to conflict?

6

MANAGING THE POWER ARENA

W HILE PERCEPTIONS OF POWER ARE PIVOTAL IN ALL CONFLICTS, POWER issues seem to loom larger in organizational conflicts. Since the workplace seems to magnify power issues, we will address the issues and challenges of managing and balancing power in some detail.

Managing the power arena in organizational disputes involves several elements: balancing interpersonal power in the negotiation, breaking any deadlocks that occur and softening and re-configuring coalitions.

Balancing Interpersonal Power

In destructive conflicts, players get snared into repetitive rounds of dirty tactics largely because each feels the other has more power or influence, as Joyce Hocker and William Wilmot explain.[1] The global arms race is a classic example of this destructive pattern. With every move one makes, the other feels behind and then escalates, not simply to catch up, but to move to the next level. Both keep escalating to try to create safety and to try to win. Disputants attempting to match each other's power create a never-ending spiral of moves and countermoves.

Even when the formal distribution of power is disparate — between a supervisor and employee, for example — typically *both* parties feel frustrated, low in power and unable to accomplish their goals. Although supervisors have the most apparent and obvious power, they often make low-power statements such as, "I just can't get people to cooperate and it is driving me crazy."

The focus on power flows directly out of their frustration. When they are feeling blocked by others, people leap to the erroneous conclusion that increasing their power would settle the conflict. In fact, just the reverse is true. The best single indicator that a conflict is nearing resolution is when the whole power issue quietly recedes into the background. Once you begin to balance power enough to get the participants to cooperate, they will voluntarily begin focusing on issues other than power and influence. Actually, *until* you can help them to alter their perceptions and to feel they can meet their interests by cooperating, they will be caught in the spiral of power struggles.

Mediators can exercise considerable influence on power plays by (1) creating boundaries for the mediation, (2) limiting the influence of the high-power party, (3) increasing the influence of the low-power party and (4) transcending the win/lose structure of the conflict.

Creating boundaries

This means setting limits to parties' actions, creating an atmosphere of cooperation and safety. There are a number of things to do at the outset to help balance power and/or get the participants to resist power struggles. First, as noted earlier, you agree to ground rules that work to balance power. Giving each person equal talk time is a good example of power balancing: "Thanks, John, for that clear statement. Now let's give Jan equal time to relate her experience of this struggle."

By setting a tone of respect and consideration, you model the importance of treating each other with respect. You can also communicate equality non-verbally — by sitting equally close to both people, using the same tone of voice when talking to everyone, attending equally to what each is saying and looking at both people equally throughout the mediation. Verbally and non-verbally, the basic message to communicate is, "I am in the middle, balancing the forces between the two of you, to help you manage this dispute. I work for the overall relationship, not for either of you individually, and I will insist on settings and situations that allow you both equal impact in the outcome of this conflict."

In addition, make certain there are no caucuses or other private talks unless all are aware of them. Having set a tone of consideration, balance and safety for both parties, you can then move to balance power at even deeper levels.

Limiting the influence of high-power parties

All people caught in destructive conflict cycles see themselves as low in power, yet, in organizations, one person usually has more official power. Because of this power discrepancy, those lower in the organizational structure need some safety guarantees. Frightened people do not negotiate well. By setting limits on the higher-power person, you reduce fear, enabling those with lower power to practice productive conflict.

Those in high power can be restrained, first of all, by *having them agree to stop destructive moves*. When entering an organizational dispute, a basic requirement is getting the official, higher-power person to exercise voluntarily restraints. We begin by saying something like this: "Obviously, this is an important conflict and you are frustrated by it. However, if your employees are feeling threatened, they can't work with you on solving it. As you know, your employees are very dependent upon you, so they will need some reassurances before they will be able to work this out with you. We suggest you send a memo or have a meeting where you announce that we are going to work this conflict through, and promise to take no personnel action for six months in order to give this process a chance to work for all concerned."

Other kinds of assurances regarding performance reviews, work on projects, support with other employees or the supervisor's future accessibility may also be required. The lower-power party can tell the mediator what kinds of assurance he or she needs. A question like, "What is your worst fear about participating in this mediation?" usually elicits information about areas where protection is needed.

Whether orally or in writing, assurances of restraint bind the higher-power person to a productive process and also protect people from precipitous action such as being fired or demoted. This changes the structure of the relationship giving the parties more equal footing.

As a conflict develops, the higher-power person will withdraw, try to establish independence and protect him/herself from the relationship with the lower-power person. Such moves to assert independence only serve to frustrate the lower-power person.

Paradoxically, the higher-power person produces more productive responses from the lower-power person by *opening up more to their influence*. Meeting with others, asking for their help and including them in decisions will both limit the power of the higher-power person and simultaneously nudge the lower-power person into more productive behavior.

At the heart of all power issues is dependence.[2] Those we depend upon are powerful to us. We have power only if others are dependent upon something we have or have access to. Thus, *you can limit higher-power parties by increasing their dependence on the lower-power person.* Let's look at how this may work.

Increasing the influence of lower-power parties

Power balancing also can come from the other side, by increasing the power of the lower-power person. Lower-power parties can become more influential if they (1) are reminded of the influence they already exert, (2) can decrease their dependence on those with higher power, (3) can form coalitions with others when needed or (4) can increase their value to the higher-power person, thus increasing the latter's dependence on them.

Chapter 1 includes a sample dialogue from a situation where power played a role. The new executive director discovered that the woman in charge of cleaning also had a strong web of relationships and connections that gave her enormous power in the organization. Without her support, the new director would have a difficult time implementing any of his programs. Reminding her of her influence set the stage for productive negotiations, calming her fears while also making the director aware that it was in his own best interest to negotiate in good faith with her.

Increasing the available alternatives decreases dependence and thus helps to balance the power, as another conflict demonstrated. An environmental group was pushing hard on a governmental agency whose director would not provide information needed to settle the dispute. Frustration at not being able to impact a high-power agency led to name-calling and attacks. Reminding the group in caucus that there were other avenues for getting the information they needed de-escalated the conflict. Interestingly, when one group stopped name-calling, the other group became more cooperative.

Sometimes lower-power parties need to form coalitions with other groups or other sources of outside influence just to get the attention of the higher-power parties. When a city wanted to negotiate with a developer regarding land use, the developer refused to come to the table — until the city discovered an ordinance that legally required the developer to jointly design the project.

The higher-power parties sometimes need to be reminded of the value of the lower-power party. Managers can be reminded that they need the goodwill of their subordinates, the expertise of certain team members and the approval and acceptance of their team. Developers need some regard from the community if their projects are to be accepted and not fought in the courts.

Oftentimes, reminding the lower-power person that the higher-power person does, in fact, need things from them unfreezes the conflict enough to produce movement.

Productive power balancing moves require that the mediator and the lower-power disputant understand what is important for the higher-power party, both on the content and relational levels. Productive power balancing is done from the perspective of knowing and meeting peoples' needs, not blocking them. In destructive conflict, both sides try to exert their own needs and block the others, creating the familiar negative spiral. The mediator moves to reverse the spiral by using knowledge of the other supportively.

Transcending win/lose structures

One way to transcend win/lose structures is by *inducing the parties to reinvest in their relationship with each other*. Just as their distress springs from their relationship, so the resolution also comes from within the context of their relationship. Reinvesting involves both parties stopping destructive moves, realizing their needs for one another and recognizing the cooperative moves the others are making to prevent the conflict from worsening. Pointing out how the disputants are being cooperative with one another and changing some of their negative moves helps to change the win/lose pattern.

Helpful statements that reinforce new patterns include:

- ▸ I appreciate your listening to each other.

- ▸ You were able to agree on this issue so I know we can resolve others.

- ▸ He cooperated with you on that issue so I know I can expect your cooperation on the next one.

- ▸ You all have played by the ground rules, which has allowed us to move along more quickly than I first expected. Thank you.

Another way to break the win/lose spiral is to re-frame the parties' views of each other.

Alan says, "He is just trying to control me. Did you hear that threat he made?" You intervene by re-framing his statement, "He must really be at his wit's end about how to deal with you if he has to resort to threats." Re-framing is discussed in detail in Chapter 3, pages 134-138.

Combine any and all the techniques discussed here to halt destructive power moves and align the parties as people invested in finding a constructive outcome.

Breaking Deadlocks

The department head says, "I just will not agree to his request for reclassification, no matter what," and the employee says, "I refuse to satisfy her need for power until she reclassifies me." Deadlock! A deadlock is when the parties freeze into their respective positions.

Deadlocks arise for reasons. Generally, it's because people want to maintain a sense of power and/or want to prevent what's perceived as a loss. More specifically, there are some key reasons people deadlock and possible responses mediators can make to re-focus the conflict.

Treat deadlocks as just another event in the unfolding conflict and remember you have a variety of ways to unlock the conflict and move the participants from their rigid stances. The objective is to loosen the deadlock so those in conflict can return to productive negotiations. This means the disputants must discover a more compelling reason to move from their rigid positions than to stay stuck. Much of the work of breaking deadlocks involves both re-framing and continuously tapping into the best of people — their caring, their understanding, their ability to empathize and see where the other party is coming from.

Why Deadlocks Happen

Reason	*Response*
Disputants are hopeless, feeling despair.	▸ Remain optimistic: "I think we can work this out." ▸ Express appreciation for the parties: "I thought you'd have horns, but you are nice people." ▸ Express hope: "I see many commonalities and options here."
Hidden payoffs for staying in conflict, such as blocking the other, getting even, predictability or the desire to win.	▸ Remind the parties they do not have the power to force the issue: "You act as if you have the ability to control the conflict, but it is my understanding the other side also has the power to block your goals." ▸ Remind the parties of what they stand to lose by deadlocking and what they can gain by negotiating. ▸ Indicate that the other party can and will go further than anticipated if blocked, e.g., to legal action, community activism, etc.
Power is obtained by resisting. Often lower-power parties get attention when they are resisting. But higher-power parties can resist, hoping to wear down the opposition.	▸ Confront the higher-power parties with the need to attend the mediation process to reduce resistance. ▸ Demonstrate positive ways of gaining power versus the negative consequences of blocking. ▸ Remind the higher-power parties of the long-term consequences of resistance, i.e., negative forces tend to build up and produce worse conflicts in the future. ▸ Help lower-power parties to find other sources of power or build coalitions to sustain them.

and How to Handle Them

	▸ Highlight the negative pattern of ignoring, resisting and anger. Sometimes this will encourage people to self-monitor.
	▸ Have one side realize how important certain goals are to the other side. Often, if there is a basis of caring or any kind of positive relationship, this demonstration of importance can break the deadlock.
Fear of loss: Substantive and relational.	▸ Indicate that many losses are already occurring and that resistance may lead to more loss than gain.
	▸ Help the parties learn to let go in order to get better choices or to reduce damage.
	▸ Offer or construct ways for the participants to feel more protected.
	▸ Demonstrate how they can minimize losses and maximize gains.
Resistance meets psychological needs, i.e., participants don't want to be embarrassed, want to gain power, want to look competent.	▸ Show how they can meet the same needs in more positive ways.
	▸ Stroke participants for their positive attributes and actions: "I appreciate your willingness to be flexible; I admire your ability to solve complex problems in the heat of conflict."
There is a clash of important values, and participants see no way to compromise values.	▸ Ignore a discussion of values and focus on interests.
	▸ Find a common value that transcends the conflicting ones.
	▸ Remind the participants of significant others who want a settlement: people they care about, value, respect or who have power over their important goals.

Softening Coalitions

The presence of coalitions has a direct bearing on managing conflict in organizations. In fact, as conflicts intensify, coalitions become more rigid, destructive and toxic.

It is normal for people to spend time together, share information and support one another in small sub-groups. And as they do, they form coalitions. A coalition forms whenever you spend more time with some people than others, whenever you exclude others and whenever you begin to criticize those who are not in your group.

We believe coalitions begin for good reasons and that coalitions are self-justifying — as is isolation from a coalition.

As you begin spending more time with Allen rather than Ron, you begin to like Allen more, see him as a potential friend and slowly form closer ties. This gradually becomes self-justifying: "We are close because he is a really neat guy." At the same time, you begin to share the imperfections you notice in those with whom you don't spend time: "Wow, wouldn't it be strange to be married to someone like Larry? He is just fundamentally weird." Thus a coalition begins to form.

Similarly, as others form coalitions and exclude us, we tend to justify being isolated from them. When someone says, "Well, I just don't want to go to lunch with such a group of gossipers," they are justifying their own isolation from the coalition. Both the presence of a coalition and isolation from coalitions tend to increase and spiral over time. Those "in" grow even closer and those "out" become even more isolated.

In addition, countercoalitions form and then begin to struggle against one another. Soon you find that a coalition, which may have begun as an answer to the problem of isolation, for example, has become the problem.

As groups vie for influence and cause difficulties for one another, the workplace degenerates into "us – them" factions. New employees are told quietly, "You better be careful which group you join here. It will determine your future in the company." Unresolved conflicts continue to escalate and become more toxic over time. Coalitions we have seen assume an "us – them" destructive pattern include:

- New employees vs. those who began with the company.
- Members of an extended family vs. those not related to them.
- Smokers vs. non-smokers.
- Males vs. females.
- Straights vs. gays.
- Caucasians vs. minorities.
- Mid-level management vs. everyone else.

Coalitions are so important that you can predict the organizational conflicts based only on the coalitions. As soon as you can ask who is "in" and who is "out," the coalitions are seen and you know what problems will emerge. Consider Wayne, who supervises four people, but only one of them, Frank, is his fishing buddy. Undoubtedly the three excluded employees will form a coalition and will be in conflict at some point with Wayne or Frank.

Coalitions are best dealt with by altering the communication patterns, by doing what is *unnatural.*

Bring together people who would normally avoid one another and help them recognize and develop joint interests. There may be some initial conflict that may have to be mediated, but a common stake in product development, or even organizing a company picnic, for example, may help form new communication links.

Deep, fundamental differences, whether perceived or real — like those around gender, race and sexual preference — require devoting a great deal of time to developing an understanding of the other's reality. As a first step, we often ask the two groups to generate questions of each other and then listen to each other's stories about their experiences of being in the organization.

In such situations, men often ask women what they would do to change the way teams work and how they would improve productivity.

Men want to know what makes the women feel low-power in the organization, or how they want men to respond when they cry. Women ask how men feel about traveling with women colleagues, what is risky about standing up for social justice issues at work and what women lose by working eighty hours a week. Careful listening to the women's answers gives both men and women important information about working together.

The rules of asking questions and then listening for clarity — not for argument — must be strictly adhered to. Often this can produce a kind of heartful listening that opens the way to real, *human* connection.

When people avoid one another, misunderstandings and discord grow. Strained and problematic relationships can be healed only by finding something in common — and that can only be discovered through direct communication.

A wise manager does not allow rigid coalitions to form. Re-shuffling work groups, building department-wide teams, supporting and insisting on genuine dialogue among different groups and any other ways that can keep working patterns dynamic will help employees form multiple links and build a healthier organization in the process.

Balancing power can go well beyond settling immediate conflicts. When people realize they have power and a fair chance to influence a conflict, they begin to use their creativity, their energy and their general goodwill in service of productive, mutually beneficial outcomes. Managing the power arena, both interpersonally and organizationally, can enhance the workplace and working relationships to everyone's benefit.

EPILOGUE:
MEDIATION AS ART

WHILE MEDIATION IS BOTH A SCIENCE AND AN ART, THIS BOOK HAS focused primarily on the science, detailing the steps in the process, providing real life examples and giving you the tools we have found useful in practicing mediation.

But what of the art, the nuances, the moment-to-moment judgments that can tip the tension of a conflict toward reconciliation rather than rupture? What does that spring from?

In brief, the artfulness is what you bring to the process and what you give of yourself. It arises from your having prepared yourself so thoroughly that you are free to allow creative responses to bubble to the surface in the heat of conflict. Such self-preparation is not a stage to be arrived at but a process, a continuous journey of discovery. As you spiral to ever deeper levels of understanding on your journey, we offer you some truths that we find are central to artful mediation.

We Are All Connected

The implications of this one are vast. First, consider how each participant in a conflict is connected with him or herself — in mind, body and spirit. Being aware of these different levels or aspects allows you to watch for cues about people's feelings as a dispute unfolds and subtle indicators about whether or not agreements will work because of a person's internal issues. We use the "Blip Theory" of diagnosis to begin to recognize and approach these various levels.

Connection also means that, unless an agreement addresses all parts of the person, it likely will not stick. They must think it is workable, feel it is equitable and believe that the agreed-upon solution will be in their best, higher interests, that the agreement is not simply an expedient answer but is the right thing to do. Normally in most organizational contexts, concerns of the spirit are routinely overlooked. People are neither invited nor encouraged to express their feelings and are often seen as weak if any emotional expressions slip out. There are even stronger taboos about questioning whether solutions are the right thing ethically, or for the good of the whole, or for the good of the human spirit. This is in sharp contrast to the Native American tradition which recognizes interconnectedness and requires asking what the impact of any change or decision will be in the future.

As a mediator, you must be willing to be spirit guardians and the voice of future generations, to watch for and to include all the aspects of each individual, even those that are not being discussed. Only when the spoken and unspoken are congruent within each person will agreements stick and their positive human energy be transformed.

Another implication of interconnectedness is that you and the participants are interdependent. From one perspective, a mediator should be seen as neutral or impartial. That is true in the sense that both parties should be able to trust the mediator to be on both their sides. At a more subtle level, however, the energy the mediator brings is a key element in reconciliation. When you are able to see through the destructiveness of people's actions to their whole, essentially positive natures, you can be instrumental in helping them move toward cooperation.

When you speak to the best in people — and expect the best from them — you often get it. If you don't address it, you rarely will.

Balancing Body, Mind and Spirit
Helps You Listen with Compassion

Then there is the matter of your own interconnectedness. It is difficult for unbalanced people to mediate balanced solutions. We find it essential to focus on the relationship of our own mind, body and spirit. We believe that the self is the change agent and know that your mental state can actually strengthen the people you work with and help produce hope between them. We each have our own ways of preparing ourselves to bring the mind, body and spirit into alignment for mediation. While meditating, Bill often pictures himself with his arms outstretched, holding each person in his hands. He assures them he is working for them both and for their relationship and that he is committed to maintaining the balance to the best of his ability. Elaine does visioning exercises, sending light, a universal symbol of empowerment, to all the parties. She is also a runner, and uses that as a sort of moving meditation, paying attention to see if she is hurrying to get to the next marker, for example. Then she knows to pay particular attention to her tendency to rush into too rapid an agreement.

You may already have your own ways of centering so that you can listen with openness and compassion. If not, we urge you to talk with others about centering and clearing techniques and continue exploring until you find what works for you. These techniques are an integral part of balancing the art with the science and are always addressed in our classes on mediation.

In addition, you need to recognize that your own personal growth is an ongoing process that will aid your mediation work. Examining your biases and identifying your fears, emotional triggers and hot buttons will help keep them from blocking your clear perception of others. As the mediation wheel suggests, the process moves from a soft to a hard perspective, from entry to diagnosis around to follow-up. In much the same way, you need to develop both your soft and your hard sides, your ability to listen and be compassionate as well as your ability to be precise and methodical and hold people accountable.

Cooperation Catalyzes Creativity

Another aspect of your task as mediator is to look for and help the participants find cooperative solutions — creative ways to link people and answers to their problems, alternatives that allow efforts to be reduced and innovation enhanced, by having people work together, not singly. Such solutions, sometimes called integrative, can provide surprise and delight. Carol Gilligan, a social scientist from Harvard, gave a wonderful example of an integrative solution that involved two kids playing.[1] The little boy wanted to play pirate; the little girl, house. First they argued about who would win, wasting their time to play together. Then they settled on playing pirates who live next door to each other, a solution that integrates both their interests. Lest you dismiss this as only a childlike solution, far too naive for the competitive, adult world, consider the recent changes in South Africa. The nation's move from apartheid to democracy has come as a white man, F. W. de Klerk, gave up more than he had to and a black man, Nelson Mandela, took less than he could have taken.[2]

Constructive conflict, whether among friends, colleagues, factions or nations is not for the faint of heart. It requires what was once called gumption to maintain hope and bring forth the vision to see cooperative solutions — a combination of perseverance, forgiveness and integration.

Contemporary companies are increasingly facing and embracing a paradox: They can only gain a competitive advantage when they focus on building cooperative partnerships. These emerging partnerships may sometimes involve old enemies and other times include new players. But companies thrive once they have succeeded in re-framing the old union-management adversarial stances into partnerships that embrace common goals that serve both the individual workers and the company as a whole. High tech giants continue healthy growth by looking for ways to cooperate with other companies so that each is not required to have all the expertise or produce all the components essential for their products. Hospitals seek ways to cooperate so that each is not required to have all the specialized treatment centers or every enormously expensive new piece of diagnostic equipment. Human Resources divisions on various sites of a company are centralizing in regions and, more dramatically, are creating pan-continental networks of consultants and specialists, so that expertise does not have to be replicated at each site and corporate wheels reinvented each time a new venture comes along.

These connected, cooperative solutions require examining our beliefs about the very nature of accomplishment and strength. Our culture is based on an assumption that it's the best people who do it on their own, without any help from others. We are used to operating from this assumption without even being aware of its existence. But it is important to realize that this represents a cultural legacy, not something innate about human nature. Often it's when different cultures come together that the implicit assumptions are brought forth.

There's a story about a group of soccer coaches who set about teaching the game to a group of Maori children, the indigenous people of New Zealand. The kids took to the game with great enthusiasm and loved moving the ball down the field and scoring goals. The only problem was that somehow they arranged it so that both teams made the same score. Competition was so alien an idea that the Maori children simply skipped right over it and went directly to having a good time, leaving their coaches dumbfounded.

The future cultures will be ones where the best people seek cooperative linkages and partnerships to solve complex problems in a whirlwind world of change. Czech President Vaclav Havel recently delivered a sort of declaration of interdependence, noting that

Western culture has reached a phase where "everything is possible and almost nothing is certain." He called for a shared global vision that enables diverse peoples, multi-cultural societies and competing religions to transcend their particularities in order to address the deepest issues of our continued existence.[3]

As we begin shifting any of our basic assumptions, conflict usually emerges. Mediation has an important message here — that cooperative processes produce greater commitment and better solutions, no matter how complex the problems.

Storytelling in Safety Produces Movement

This truth is grounded in understanding that most people have few or no ways to tell their truth in a safe place, where power is balanced. A major part of mediation is both allowing and encouraging participants to tell their piece of the truth, without judging or being judged, so that all involved feel affirmed. Storytelling, in addition to silence, song and dance, are the key ways that people heal and prosper, according to Angeles Arrien, an anthropologist who specializes in cross-cultural education.[4] As people tell their stories to someone receptive, all who share in the experience begin to find common ground, see ways in which they are different but not in conflict and identify the specific problem areas that must be worked out. Understanding the context within which another person lives and works allows creative solutions to arise, ideas that are compatible with the needs of all the people involved.

Storytelling is being used in a variety of settings where there is overt or covert conflict. In multi-cultural work, for example, women, men and those of different racial, religious or ethnic groups listen without interruption to each other's experiences of the workplace. There is no intention of fixing the problem or probing with questions, but merely to hear how another experiences a situation. Another's experience often proves to be very different from what you thought to be true. This process, which Julian Weissglass calls "constructivist listening," tends to lead to empathy, compassion and ultimately to solutions that grow out of a deep understanding of the other and a trust within which dialogue can occur.[5] Over and over again mediation work reveals that you do not have to know the solutions to all the problems. The process itself provides the answers. Through dialogue contained in safety, people's strengths and abilities emerge so that, together, complex issues can be solved. We have often experienced that expression plus connection equals transformation.

Doubtless there are many other truths from your background that you can bring to support successful mediation. Our aim is to remind you that the fullness of who you are makes a difference, and the more you can bring of yourself to managing conflict and mediating disputes, the more artful you will become. May you find the process inspiring.

NOTES

Introduction

1. This concept is both specified and expanded by William L. Ury, Jeanne M. Brett and Stephen B. Goldberg in *Getting Disputes Resolved: Designing Systems to Cut the Costs of Conflict* (San Francisco: Jossey-Bass, 1988), 11.

2. Hudson Institute, *Workforce 2000: Competing in a Seller's Market* (Valhalla, N.Y.: Towers Perrin, 1990). See also David Jamison and Julie O'Mara, *Managing Workforce 2000: Gaining the Diversity Advantage* (San Francisco: Jossey-Bass, 1991).

3. Anthony F. Buono and James L. Bowditch, *The Human Side of Mergers and Acquisitions: Managing Coalitions Between People, Cultures, and Organizations* (San Francisco: Jossey-Bass, 1989), 7 and 10.

4. Adapted from Steve Leas and Paul Kittlaus, *Church Fights: Managing Conflict in the Local Church* (Philadelphia: Westminster Press, 1973), 65-72.

Chapter 1

1.   How to Handle Grief and Loss in Conflict*

Stages of Grieving	Appropriate Responses
Anger: Everything from grumbling to rage, often misdirected or undirected. Can lead to foot-dragging, "mistakes," and even sabotage.	Listen, acknowledge that the anger is understandable. Don't take on the blame if it is being improperly directed toward you. Distinguish between acceptable feelings and unacceptable, acting-out behavior: "I understand how you feel, but I'm not going to let you mess up the project."
Bargaining: Unrealistic attempts to get out of the situation or to make it go away; trying to strike a special deal; making big promises to "save you a bundle of money" or "double the output" if only you'll undo the change.	Distinguish these efforts from real problem solving; keep a realistic outlook and don't be swayed by desperate arguments and impossible promises.
Anxiety: Silent or expressed; a realistic fear of an unknown and probably difficult future or, simply, catastrophic fantasies.	Anxiety is natural, so don't make people feel stupid for feeling it. Just keep feeding them the information as it comes and commiserate with them when it doesn't.

Sadness: Everything from silence to tears — the heart of the grieving process.

Encourage people to say what they are feeling and share your feelings, too. Don't try to reassure people with unrealistic suggestions of hope. Sympathize.

Disorientation: Confusion and forgetfulness even among organized people; feelings of being lost and insecure.

Give people extra support — opportunities to get things off their chests, reassurances that disorientation is natural and that other people feel it too. And give them extra attention.

Depression: Feeling down, flat, dead; hopelessness and constant fatigue.

Like sadness and anger, depression is hard to be around. However, you can't make it go away. People have to go through it, not around it. Make it clear that you understand and perhaps even share similar feelings yourself, but that work still needs to be done. Do whatever you can to restore people's sense of having some control over their situations.

*Adapted from *Managing Transitions* (pp. 24–25) ©1991 by William Bridges and Associates, Inc. Reprinted by permission of Addison-Wesley Publishing Company, Inc.

Chapter 2

1. Joyce Hocker and William W. Wilmot, *Interpersonal Conflict,* 4th ed. (Dubuque, Iowa: W. C. Brown, 1995).

2. Hocker and Wilmot provide a detailed explanation of the various overt and covert expressions of conflict.

3. For a full explanation and numerous case studies, see Marvin R. Weisbord (with thirty-five international co-authors), *Discovering Common Ground* (San Francisco: Berrett-Kohler Publishers, 1992). He provides both theoretical information and descriptions of the practice of reaching common ground.

4. Hocker and Wilmot, *Interpersonal Conflict.*

5. See Blue Sky Video (Blue Sky Productions, Inc., 5918 Pulaski Ave., Philadelphia, PA 19144).

6. Hocker and Wilmot, *Interpersonal Conflict.*

7. The total quality movement addresses this issue by having each function and person within the function identify and make agreements with internal suppliers and vendors to accomplish critical tasks along the work flow chain. These agreements are like small mediations all through the system and help avoid unnecessary conflict. This also prevents errors and problems from accumulating in the system, only to show up at the front end of the line and/or with customers.

8. Peter Senge, *The Fifth Discipline* (New York: Doubleday, 1990).

9. Search Conference methodology, pioneered by Marvin Weisbord, details the theory and practice of finding common ground.

10. William Ury, Jeanne M. Brett and Stephen B. Goldberg offer a detailed description of constructive conflicts in organizations in *Getting Disputes Resolved: Designing Systems to Cut the Costs of Conflict* (San Francisco: Jossey-Bass, 1988), 11.

11. Christopher Moore, *The Mediation Process* (San Francisco: Jossey-Bass, 1986).

Chapter 3

1. Agendas and formats for generations options are from Moore, 182-185.

2. These guidelines for brainstorming are adapted from Roger Fisher and William Ury, *Getting to Yes: Negotiating Agreement without Giving In* (New York: Penguin Books, 1991).

Chapter 4

1. Moore, *The Mediation Process*, 15.

2. Fisher and Ury, *Geting to Yes,* 64.

Chapter 6

1. Hocker and Wilmot, *Interpersonal Conflict.*

2. For a more complete discussion, see Richard Emerson, "Power Dependence Relations," *American Sociological Review* 21 (1962): 31-41.

Epilogue

1. Carol Gilligan, *In a Different Voice: Psychological Theory and Women's Development* (Cambridge: Harvard University Press, 1982).

2. The Reverend Cannon Peter L. Gunning from Johannesburg, South Africa, offered these words while attending work on transition management that Elaine and her husband, Mike Burr, were conducting in Lausanne, Switzerland, June 1994. Many thanks to him for his insight, humor and wonderful storytelling abilities and our profound gratitude to people like Peter all over South Africa who have devoted years to managing its heated societal disputes and who have persisted in ways filled with great integrity.

3. Quoted in the *Newsweek* report by Kenneth L. Woodward, "More Than Ourselves," July 18, 1994, 66.

4. Angeles Arrien, *The Four-Fold Way: Walking the Paths of the Warrior, Teacher, Healer and Visionary* (San Francisco: Harper San Francisco, 1993).

5. Julian Weissglass, "Constructivist Listening for Empowerment and Change," *The Educational Forum* 54, no. 4 (Summer 1990). Our thanks to Lillian Roybal Rose from Davenport, California, who conducts multi-cultural workshops for introducing us to this method. She is a master of her art.

BIBLIOGRAPHY

Arrien, Angeles. *The Four-Fold Way: Walking the Paths of the Warrior, Teacher, Healer and Visionary* (San Francisco: Harper San Francisco, 1993).

Block, Peter. *Flawless Consulting, A Guide to Getting Your Expertise Used* (Austin, Tex.: Learning Concepts, 1981).

Bridges, William. *Managing Transitions: Making the Most of Change* (Reading, Mass.: Addison-Wesley, 1991).

Buono, Anthony F., and James L. Bowditch. *The Human Side of Mergers and Acquisitions: Managing Coalitions Between People, Cultures, and Organizations* (San Francisco: Jossey-Bass, 1989).

Fisher, Roger, and William Ury. *Getting to Yes: Negotiating Agreement without Giving In.* 2nd ed. (New York: Penguin Books, 1991).

Gilligan, Carol. *In a Different Voice: Psychological Theory and Women's Development* (Cambridge, Mass.: Harvard University Press, 1982).

Hocker, Joyce, and William W. Wilmot. *Interpersonal Conflict.* 4th ed. (Dubuque, Iowa: W. C. Brown, 1995).

Hudson Institute. *Workforce 2000: Competing in a Seller's Market* (Valhalla, N.Y.: Towers Perrin, 1990).

Jamison, David, and Julie O'Mara. *Managing Workforce 2000: Gaining the Diversity Advantage* (San Francisco: Jossey-Bass, 1991).

Leas, Steve, and Paul Kittlaus. *Church Fights: Managing Conflict in the Local Church* (Philadelphia: Westminster Press, 1973).

Moore, Christopher. *The Mediation Process* (San Francisco: Jossey-Bass, 1986).

Senge, Peter. *The Fifth Discipline* (New York: Doubleday, 1990).

Ury, William L., Jeanne M. Brett and Stephen B. Goldberg. *Getting Disputes Resolved: Designing Systems to Cut the Costs of Conflict* (San Francisco: Jossey-Bass, 1988).

Weisbord, Marvin R. *Discovering Common Ground* (San Francisco: Berrett-Kohler Publishers, 1992).

Weissglass, Julian. "Constructivist Listening for Empowerment and Change." *The Educational Forum* 54, no. 4 (Summer 1990).

INDEX

221